CHOOSING YOUR

Eternal

companion

CHOOSING YOUR
Eternal
companion

Robert K. McIntosh

CFI
An Imprint of Cedar Fort, Inc.
Springville, Utah

This is not an official publication of The Church of Jesus Christ of Latter-day Saints. The opinions and views expressed herein belong solely to the authors and do not necessarily represent the opinions or views of Cedar Fort, Inc. Permission for the use of sources, graphics, and photos is also solely the responsibility of the authors.

ISBN 13: 978-1-4621-1472-6

Published by CFI, an imprint of Cedar Fort, Inc.
2373 W. 700 S., Springville, UT 84663
Distributed by Cedar Fort, Inc., www.cedarfort.com

LIBRARY OF CONGRESS CATALOGING-IN-PUBLICATION DATA ON FILE.

Cover design by Shawnda T. Craig
Cover design © 2014 Lyle Mortimer
Edited and typeset by Kevin Haws

Printed in the United States of America

10 9 8 7 6 5 4 3 2 1

Printed on acid-free paper

Dedication

To my eternal companion, Susan, who has been an example to me of each principle in the Proclamation.

Contents

Contents

Acknowledgments

I would like to thank the following for their inspiration and help with this book:

To the First Presidency and Quorum of Twelve Apostles of The Church of Jesus Christ of Latter-day Saints for the Proclamation. I hope I have not distracted in any way from this inspired document.

To William O. Nelson, for his guidance and assistance with the manuscript, especially the first chapter.

To Karleen Hamilton and Leonard Tourney, two dear friends who reviewed and gave suggestions for the manuscript.

To Catherine Christensen of Cedar Fort Publishing; if she had not visited me at BYU Education Week, this book would never have been published.

To the editors at Cedar Fort, especially Kevin Haws.

To my beloved wife, Susan, for her constant inspiration and encouragement.

Section I: Preparing to Be the Right One

Perhaps you have wondered at what age you should begin preparing to marry. Actually, you have been preparing from the day you were born. The family you were born into, the habits and attitudes you have developed, the friends you have chosen, and the decisions you have made regarding the gospel have all had an influence on your preparation.

Consider a law of life called "the law of attraction," that being you will attract the type of person that you are prepared for. (See D&C 88:40.) This section will center on specific principles from "The Family: A Proclamation to the World" that you can focus on right now to become the right one before you marry.

Chapter 1
Why This Proclamation?

Introduction

You were born in one of the most important periods in the history of this world. Prophets have said that you were reserved for this time to help prepare for the Second Coming of Jesus Christ. The devil knows this and who you are and will seek to convince you otherwise. He has saved his most enticing temptations for this generation. All around are young people and adults who have bought into his lies and falsehoods, becoming addicted to drugs, alcohol, pornography, and had marriages and families broken by adultery and divorce.

Father in Heaven wants to help you avoid these bad choices and tragic consequences. Your future depends on knowing and living what is real and true. I want you to know right from the beginning of this book that you can count on this Proclamation being true. Here's why.

The Background to the Proclamation

Standing in the LDS Conference Center on October 25, 1995, at a Relief Society general meeting, President Gordon B. Hinckley read a proclamation entitled "The Family: A Proclamation to the World" (hereafter referred to as "the Proclamation").

Perhaps you have wondered why the Proclamation was given back in 1995? Before reading the Proclamation, President Hinckley explained why it was issued at that time:

> With so much sophistry [false reasoning] that is passed off as truth, with so much of deception concerning standards and values, with so much of allurement and enticement to take on the slow stain of the

world, we have felt to warn and forewarn. In furtherance of this we of the First Presidency and the Council of the Twelve Apostles now issue a proclamation to the Church and to the world as a declaration and reaffirmation of standards, doctrines, and practices relative to the family which the prophets, seers, and revelators of this Church have repeatedly stated throughout its history.[1]

Marriage and Family Are under Attack

Let's look at what happened in the thirty-five years prior to the Proclamation to see how marriage and family were under attack. From 1960 to 1995, there was a dramatic change in marriage and in the traditional family (a husband who is the breadwinner and a wife who stays home to take care of their children), as standards and values that once protected the family unit began to deteriorate. The sixties were the point when the attack on the family intensified. I will never forget picking up a *Time* magazine while I was attending college and seeing on the cover: *God Is Dead*. Once people believed that God was dead, they felt they were free to abandon the standards of the past, venturing into "a new morality" (the old immorality).

However, we had been warned this was coming. In October 1961, at a general priesthood meeting, President Hugh B. Brown of the First Presidency issued the following prophecy and warning:

> Our purpose tonight is to warn you priesthood holders, and through you the men and women of your various groups, of the existence, strength, location, and tactics of the enemy, and to remind you that we rely on your absolute loyalty and that preparedness is indispensable. In the army too frequently we refer to fitness as only physical fitness. Tonight we are calling upon all you officers of the Church to be fit and ready, physically, mentally, morally, and spiritually, for the war that lies ahead, *because the enemy is determined to destroy all that we hold dear.*[2] (Italics added)

That last sentence could read "because the enemy is determined to destroy all that *you* hold dear." What do you hold dear that Satan will try to destroy? President Harold B. Lee indicated, "Satan's greatest threat today is to destroy the family, and to make a mockery of the law of chastity and the sanctity of the marriage covenant."[3] President Spencer W. Kimball added, "The time will come when only those who believe deeply and actively in the family will be able to preserve their families in the midst of the gathering evil around us."[4]

What Happened from the 1960s to 1995?

To understand what happened between 1960 and 1995—when the Proclamation was presented to the world—look at the rather disturbing trends in American culture relative to marriage and family that changed in those thirty-five years. As you review each of the following trends, ask yourself what impact each has had on marriage and the family unit.[5]

Trend	1960	1995	Rate of
Percentage of divorced women per 1,000	9.2%	20%	+10.8%
Number of children affected by divorce	463,000	1,000,000	+537,000
Children that are born to unmarried parents	224,300	1,253,976	+1,029,676
Couples living together without being married	493,000	3,668,000	+3,175,000
The percentage of single parents	9.1%	31%	+21.9%
Families with a male as the sole provider	42%	15%	-27%

These issues affecting the family did not occur overnight. As Alexander Pope has written, Satan uses a much more subtle approach:

> Vice is a monster of so frightful a mien [conduct],
> As to be hated needs but to be seen;
> Yet seen too oft, familiar with her face,
> We first endure, then pity, then embrace.[6]

Our Church leaders were aware of Satan's attack on marriage and the family during the years 1960–1995 and gave multiple warnings.

April 1969, President David O. McKay: "The signs of the times definitely indicate that the sacredness of the marriage covenant is dangerously threatened."[7]

November 1979, President Spencer W. Kimball: "As we look about us, we see many forces at work bent on the destruction of the family, both in America and abroad. Family ties are being destroyed by an ever-increasing divorce rate, by increased infidelity of spouses, by the abominable sin of abortion, which bids well to become a national scandal and is a very grave sin. Another erosion of the family is unwarranted and selfish birth control. The strengthening of family ties should become a rallying cry for Latter-day Saint families everywhere."[8]

1988, President Ezra Taft Benson: "The family has serious problems. Divorce is epidemic. The incidence of delinquency is on the rise. The answer is not more marriage counselors or social workers. The answer lies in a husband and wife taking their marriage covenant more seriously, realizing that they both have a responsibility to make their marriage a happy one.[9]

November 1994, President Howard W. Hunter: "A worried society now begins to see that the disintegration of the family brings upon the world the calamities foretold by the prophets. The world's councils and deliberations will succeed only when they define the family as the Lord revealed it to be."[10]

To the Women of the Church

Why did President Hinckley choose first to present the Proclamation to the women of the Church in a general Relief Society meeting? While I do not know all of the reasons, I am aware of how important he felt mothers are to the Lord's kingdom. He said,

> We must never lose sight of the strength of the women. . . . It is mothers who most directly affect the lives of our children. . . . It is mothers who nurture them and bring them up in the ways of the Lord. Their influence is paramount. . . . They are the creators of life. They are the nurturers of children. They are the teachers of young women. They are our indispensable companions. They are our co-workers in building the kingdom of God. How great is their role, how marvelous their contribution.[11]

The Purpose of This Book

You are a witness of the gradual destruction of marriages and families. Perhaps you have wondered how you can choose—let alone find—your eternal companion, and what you can do to have a happy, successful marriage. Thankfully, God has given the Proclamation as guide to you as you date and prepare you to one day marry.

The Proclamation gives you key qualities to look for in yourself and the one you are considering marrying. It can help you evaluate if both of your priorities, goals, and beliefs in life are compatible. The questions at the end of each chapter can assist you as you assess your personal preparation for marriage and give you important areas to discuss with the one whom you intend to marry. It has been said, "Keep your eyes wide open before you marry, and half shut after." The Proclamation can help you keep your eyes wide open.

How This Book Is Organized

The Proclamation consists of nine paragraphs. This book is divided into two sections. The first section is entitled *Preparing to Be the Right One*, focusing on the first five paragraphs of the Proclamation and makes up chapters 1–9 in this book. The second section is entitled *Deciding Whom to Marry* and is based on the final four paragraphs of the Proclamation, discussed in Chapters 10–20.

Each chapter begins with a chapter number and title, the paragraph number in the Proclamation, and the specific quotation from it that will be explored. (A full copy of the Proclamation can be found at https:// www.lds.org/topics/family-proclamation?lang=eng.) Normally at the conclusion of each chapter are two sections: *Questions for Thought and Discussion* and *Suggested Readings*. At the end of the book is an appendix entitled *Seven Suggestions for Choosing an Eternal Companion*.

The Proclamation was studied and prayed over by leaders of the Church, and you might consider doing the same. It is scripture and may be likened to a Liahona, a compass, or an instruction manual. Use the Proclamation as you prepare for eternal marriage and family. The Prophet Joseph Smith said, when asked how he governed such a large group of people, "I teach them correct principles and they govern themselves."[12] As you study the doctrines and principles in the Proclamation with a prayerful attitude, the Lord will guide you in applying them to your life. In fact, President Henry B. Eyring said, "As you read the Family Proclamation, the Holy Spirit can tell you it is true."[13]

Questions for Thought and Discussion

    1. How would it benefit your life now if you had a testimony that the Proclamation was inspired by God?

    2. If you do not have that testimony, how might you receive it?

Chapter 2
A Testimony of Living Prophets

Paragraph 1: We, the First Presidency and the Council of the Twelve Apostles of The Church of Jesus Christ of Latter-day Saints, solemnly proclaim . . .

Introduction

Consider this analogy: a group of young people is going down the rapids of a raging river, screaming and holding on for dear life. The current of the river is pulling them ever closer to danger. Little did those in the boat know what lay ahead—a ten-foot waterfall that, if not prepared for, could certainly injure them or even take their lives. If they had looked up, they would have seen a forest ranger standing in a tower, waving his arms and shouting, "Up ahead, look out!"

In your life, perhaps you are sailing through, enjoying your friends and family and meeting the challenges of life with the hope of a happy future. However, the current of society, with its seductive people and lifestyles, is seeking to take you into dangers waters. They are saying things like:

- Come over here with us and be happy.

- Eat, drink and be merry, for tomorrow you may die.

- Religion is for older people. Live it up now!

In the Proclamation, prophets of God, standing on higher ground, are raising a warning voice to you:

- Follow this Proclamation; its principles will help you prepare for an eternal marriage and family.

- The only safety you have in these perilous times is following the counsel of your parents and Church leaders.

Satan Is Raging in People's Hearts

The prophet Nephi in the Book of Mormon warned that in the last days Satan would rage "in the hearts of the children of men" (see 2 Nephi 28:20). The Prophet Joseph Smith was shown in vision some of the atrocities of the last days: "I saw men hunting the lives of their own sons, and brother murdering brother, women killing their own daughters, and daughters seeking the lives of their mothers. . . . Satan will rage, and the spirit of the devil is now enraged."[1]

Satan's objective is to influence you to be as miserable as he is (see 2 Nephi 2:27). Because he will never have what you can have, he seeks to deprive you of it. In the words of Elder Boyd K. Packer, "The single purpose of Lucifer is to oppose the great plan of happiness, to corrupt the purest, most beautiful and appealing experiences in life: romance, love, marriage, and parenthood."[2]

Heavenly Father Has Not Left You Alone

One of the most important decisions you face as you prepare for marriage is whom you will go to for guidance. Who is telling you the truth? Friends can give you advice, television programs and movies will condition you to think about love and marriage in certain ways, but you must decide whom you will listen to and trust.

A lesson I have learned in over thirty-eight years of teaching young people is that the Lord has not left us alone. He speaks through His prophets and apostles. Those who follow their counsel have a stronger foundation for a happy marriage than those who follow other voices.

Speaking at a general conference one year after a powerful earthquake hit off of the coast of Indonesia (creating a tsunami that killed more than 200,000 people), Elder Joseph B. Wirthlin of the Quorum of Twelve Apostles explained how one village survived without any casualties. The Moken people, a society of fishermen living off the coasts of Thailand and Burma, were taught by their ancestors how to recognize when a tsunami was coming. When an elder of the village saw the dreaded signs, he shouted for everyone to run to higher ground. Not everyone listened; one elderly fisherman said, "None of the kids believed me." In fact, his own daughter called him a liar. But the old fisherman would not give up until all had left the village and climbed to higher ground. The Moken people were spared because they listened and obeyed the old fisherman, who understood the ways of the sea. Had they not obeyed, they would have been killed. Applying a lesson from the Moken people, Elder Wirthlin said,

> Since the days of Adam, the Lord has spoken to His prophets, and while His message differs according to the specific needs of the time, there is one consistent, never-changing theme: *Depart from iniquity and journey to higher ground.* As people heed the words of the prophets, the Lord blesses them. When they disregard His word, however, distress and suffering often follow.[3] (Italics added)

The Importance of Living Prophets

Most Christians today believe that revelation from God to man ended with the Book of Revelation in the New Testament. However, the Bible itself is a tangible witness that God's pattern of revelation has continued from the beginning of creation. The Old Testament prophet Amos said concerning this pattern, "Surely the Lord God will do nothing *until* he revealeth his secrets to his servants the prophets" (JST, Amos 3:7, italics added).

The Old Testament and the Book of Mormon serve as witnesses that what Amos taught is true. For example, the Lord revealed to the prophet Noah that the world was going to be destroyed by a flood. Moses led the children of Israel out of Egyptian bondage by revelation from the Lord. Lehi was told by the Lord to leave the city of Jerusalem as it was going to fall.

President Harold B. Lee, 11th President of the Church, testified,

> Now the only safety we have as members of the Church is to do exactly what the Lord said to the Church in the day when the Church was organized. We must learn to give heed to the words and commandments that the Lord shall give through His prophet, "as he receiveth them, walking in all holiness before me; . . . as if from mine own mouth in all patience and faith (D&C 21:4–5)."[4]

A Modern Prophet

This pattern of God speaking through prophets was established in the times of the Bible and the Book of Mormon and was repeated in the year of 1820, when, after a long period of apostasy, the Lord revealed that the church He established during His mortal ministry was to be restored to the earth. Joseph Smith was called as a prophet in the same way as ancient prophets. This is the Lord's pattern and it has continued in our day since the Restoration.

President Joseph Fielding Smith gave the following promise to those who will follow the Lord's prophets: "Neither the President of the Church, nor the united voice of the First Presidency and the Twelve will ever lead the Saints astray or send forth counsel to the world that is contrary to the mind and will of the Lord."[5] (Please note that this Proclamation was given to us from the united voice of the First Presidency and the Quorum of Twelve Apostles.)

You Can Trust God's Prophets, Seers, and Revelators

Ammon in the Book of Mormon was sent by King Mosiah II from the land of Zarahemla to the land of Nephi to discover what had happened to the people of Zeniff. When Ammon found them, King Limhi asked him if he knew someone who could translate. Ammon told Limhi that King Mosiah II had that gift from God because he was not only a prophet, but he was also a seer. He then said,

> A seer is a revelator and a prophet also; and a gift which is greater can no man have, except he should possess the power of God, which no man can; yet a man may have great power given him from God, but a seer can know things which are past, and also *of things which are to come*, and by them shall all things be revealed . . . therefore, he [a seer] becometh a great benefit to his fellow beings. (Mosiah 8:16–18; italics added)

Conclusion

Right now you have fifteen prophets, seers, and revelators (the First Presidency and the Quorum of the Twelve Apostles) who have given you this Proclamation, and it will be a "great benefit" to you if you choose to pray about and follow their counsel. When our prophets, seers, and revelators gave us the Proclamation, they saw the "tsunami of evil" coming and knew what the devil would do to destroy marriages and families. The Proclamation gives you the Lord's blueprint for safety in these dangerous troubling times.

You may to choose to follow the Lord's prophets or do your own thing. President Gordon B. Hinckley said, "How grateful, my brethren, I feel . . . [that members,] when facing a major decision on which the Church has taken a stand, align themselves with that position. . . . Each of us has to face the matter—either the Church is true, or it is a fraud. There is no middle ground. It is the Church and kingdom of God, or it is nothing."[6] Either they are God's prophets or they are not.

Questions for Thought and Discussion

1. Why can you trust the counsel of our prophets, seers, and revelators?

2. What evidence have you seen in the scriptures that the words of prophets are always fulfilled?

Suggested Reading

"Singles and the Proclamation on the Family," *Ensign*, January, 2004.

Richard G. Scott, "First Things First," *Ensign*, April, 2001.

Chapter 3
An Eternal Perspective

Paragraph 1: Marriage between a man and a woman is ordained of God.

Introduction

After over fifty years of marriage, I can truthfully say I love being married to my wife, Susan. We met at Church during our high school years, dated, and after my mission were married in the Salt Lake Temple. Since then, we have faced many challenges and trials, but our love for each other has continually grown and deepened. In spite of the negative things you might have heard about marriage, I know it can be one of the most joyful and enriching experiences of life.

This chapter will focus on why marriage between a man and a woman is ordained of God. As said by John and Kimberly Bytheway, "You must not only be committed to the one you marry, you must be committed to the doctrine that marriage is ordained of God."[1]

A Mortal or Eternal Perspective?

There are two basic perspectives people use when looking at dating, marriage, and family: one is a mortal perspective and the other an eternal perspective. Perspective refers to the way we look at and value things in our lives. We might compare these two perspectives to eyeglasses, through which we see the world. With mortal glasses, we see life from birth to death and base our decisions on human reasoning while rejecting revelation and spiritual things. The eternal perspective—based on revelation from God to prophets—is found in the restored gospel and views mortal life as a part of an eternal existence from the past to the future.

How can this eternal perspective given by prophets be of benefit to you? Elder Merrill J. Bateman said, "A view of marriage and the family based on eternal principles increases the probability of success. When one takes the long view [eternal perspective], one tries harder to be patient, long-suffering, kind, gentle, and meek. These characteristics, in turn, strengthen the marriage."[2]

God's Divine Plan

Perhaps you have heard things like, "Why do you want to get married? It is just a piece of paper." Or, "We don't need marriage. We can just live together." Such people either do not understand what God has said about marriage or they don't want to believe Him.

In the Creation, God created Adam. Genesis 2:15 says, "And the Lord God took the man, and put him into the garden of Eden to dress it and to keep it." In the Garden, Adam was alone, without any friends or family. But the Lord soon fixed that. "And the Lord God said, It is not good that man should be alone; I will make him an help meet for him" (Genesis 2:18). So God gave to Adam a woman whom He named Eve and God married them for time and eternity in the Garden of Eden. When Adam was alone, he was incomplete. He needed a partner, a yin for yang. Thus the Lord established the divine pattern of marriage between a man and a woman.

This divine pattern continued throughout the Old Testament and into the New Testament. The Apostle Paul taught that "neither is man without the woman nor woman without the man in the Lord" (I Corinthians 11:1).

Speaking of the importance of the duality of man and woman, President Gordon B. Hinckley said, "Man and woman are His creations. There is no other arrangement that meets the divine purposes of the Almighty. Their duality is His design. Their complementary relationships and functions are fundamental to His purposes. One is incomplete without the other."[3]

Elder Tad R. Callister explained that this duality prepares us for eternal life. "Earthly marriage is a prototype, a pattern of heavenly marriage. It is a preparation for the celestial state of affairs of which the Lord spoke: 'And that same sociality which exists among us here will exist among us there, only it will be coupled with eternal glory, which glory we do not now enjoy (D&C 130:2)."[4]

Jesus Taught the Importance of Marriage

The Proclamation states that "marriage between a man and a woman is *ordained* of God" (italics added). The word *ordained* means "to establish or order by appointment, decree, or law." In other words, in the beginning, God decreed that marriage between a man and a woman was the established order and law.

There is no clearer evidence of this divine pattern than the one given by Christ in Mark chapter 10 of the New Testament. A group of Pharisees challenged the Lord about the Law of Moses, which allowed a man to put away his wife by giving her a bill of divorcement. Jesus responded by saying that Moses allowed this because of the hardness of the people's hearts, but it was not always that way (Mark 10:2–5). The Lord then said,

> But from the beginning of the creation God made them male and female. For this cause shall a man leave his father and mother, and cleave to his wife; and they twain [two] shall be one flesh: so then they are no more twain [two], but one flesh. What therefore God hath joined together [man and woman], let no man put asunder [apart]. (Mark 10:6–9)

Elder Boyd K. Packer explained why this pattern of male and female is so important.

> The plan of happiness requires the righteous union of male and female, man and woman, husband and wife. Doctrines teach us how to respond to the compelling natural impulses which too often dominate how we behave. A body patterned after the image of God was created for Adam, and he was introduced into the Garden. At first, Adam was alone. He held the priesthood, but alone, he could not fulfill the purpose of his creation. No other man would do. Neither alone nor with other men could Adam progress. Nor could Eve with another woman. It was so then. It is so today.[5]

Marriage has been a great blessing to me because my wife and I complement each other. She is strong in areas that I am weak in and vice versa. For instance, I have noticed many times when Susan was more sensitive to the feelings of our children than I was. For us, marriage is a mutual improvement relationship.

The Proclamation establishes Heavenly Father's will concerning marriage. It therefore becomes a protection from the false philosophies of the world promoted by the devil, who is the father of all lies.

Prepare Yourself to Marry

Prophets have consistently encouraged the youth to prepare to marry. President Howard W. Hunter taught that marriage is a priesthood responsibility. "As a matter of priesthood responsibility, a man, under normal circumstances, should not unduly postpone marriage. Brethren, the Lord has spoken plainly on this matter. It is your sacred responsibility to follow His counsel and the words of His prophets."[6]

President Monson in the April 2011 General Conference said, "I have thought a lot lately about you young men who are of an age to marry but who have not yet felt to do so. I see lovely young ladies who desire to be married and to raise families, and yet their opportunities are limited because so many young men are postponing marriage."

President Monson then addressed two major reasons Latter-day Saints are postponing marriage and gave a solution for each one:

Reason: Concerns about providing financially for a wife and family.

Solution: "There is no shame in a couple scrimping and saving. It is generally during these challenging times that you will grow closer together as you learn to sacrifice and to make difficult decisions."

Reason: Fear of making the wrong choice.

Solution: "Exercise faith. Find someone with whom you can be compatible. Realize that you will not be able to anticipate every challenge which may arise, but be assured that almost anything can be worked out if you are resourceful and if you are committed to making your marriage work."[7]

Beware of Two of Satan's Greatest Lies

The Book of Mormon teaches us that the devil "is the father of all lies" (2 Nephi 2:18). Many young people today, if they are not careful, could make some serious mistakes by believing his lies.

One of his greatest lies is it doesn't matter who you date and have as friends, for when you choose to marry you can find a good Latter-day Saint and marry in the temple.

President Ezra Taft Benson said, "Don't trifle away your happiness by involvement with someone who cannot take you worthily to the temple. Make a decision now that this is the place where you will marry. To leave that decision until a romantic involvement develops is to take a risk the importance of which you cannot now fully calculate."[8] The truth is that you will marry those people you choose to date and associate yourself with.

Another great lie the devil spreads is even if the one you want to marry is not a member of your faith, you can convert them after being married. While there are exceptions to the rule, the truth is that the likelihood of a spouse joining the Church is like playing Russian roulette. Elder Robert D. Hales of the Quorum of the Twelve Apostles has given this warning: "If you marry somebody who is antagonistic to the Church or passive, . . . you are placing yourself in a position where you will find, someday, that you will have to choose between that individual and The Church of Jesus Christ."[9] Therefore, if you want a happy marriage, be careful whom you date and thereafter choose to marry.

Elder M. Russell Ballard of the Quorum of Twelve Apostles, said that the Proclamation "[is] a stern warning in a world where declining values and misplaced priorities threaten to destroy society by undermining its basic unit."[10]

What Can You Do Now to Prepare for Marriage?

- Trust in the Lord and in His prophets, and know that marriage is important and that you can be successful and happy.

- Prepare yourself by becoming the right one. For example, the more mentally and emotionally stable you are before marriage the better. Also, resolve health issues, if possible, that could cause problems in marriage.

- Place yourself in situations where you can meet and date active, committed Latter-day Saints. Some of the best places, if you do not go to a Church school, are institute or a singles ward.

- Date people who have similar standards to yours.

- Follow the counsel in the booklet "For the Strength of Youth."

- When you meet someone with whom you want to spend eternity, set aside your fears and have the faith to marry. Elder David A.

Bednar testified, "The doctrine of the plan [of salvation] leads men and women to hope and prepare for eternal marriage, and it defeats the fears and overcomes the uncertainties that may cause some individuals to delay or avoid marriage."[11]

What about those who may not marry in this life? Elder Boyd K. Packer has written,

> Now a word to those who want to love and to be loved who are slipping past the usual age for marriage. I am thinking of many of these lovely, worthy sisters who feel that life is passing them by. Unfortunately, you sometimes feel that way when you are nineteen. These suggestions: Do not give up. Hold to your standards. It may well come to you as a September song and be twice more precious for the waiting. Stay attractive—and I do not mean the cover-girl appeal—but attractive in disposition and in attitude and in service. Stay available. Do not be so content with what you do that you cease to care. To some it may not come, but surely there is a compensation that the Lord has in store for the righteous who have held to His standards, but who remain unmarried through no choice of their own.[12]

And what about divorce? President James E. Faust:

> Those marriages performed in our temples, meant to be eternal relationships, then, become the most sacred covenants we can make. . . . What, then, might be a "just cause" for breaking the covenants of marriage? Over a lifetime of dealing with human problems, I have struggled to understand what might be considered "just cause" for breaking of covenants. . . . Only the parties to the marriage can determine this. They must bear the responsibility for the train of consequences which inevitably follow if these covenants are not honored. In my opinion, "just cause" should be nothing less serious than a prolonged and apparently irredeemable relationship which is destructive of a person's dignity as a human being. At the same time, I have strong feelings about what is not provocation for breaking the sacred covenants of marriage. Surely it is not simply "mental distress," nor "personality differences," nor having "grown apart," nor having "fallen out of love." This is especially so where there are children.[13]

Conclusion

The most important decision you will make while on this earth is whom you choose to marry. Heavenly Father has given you agency to make this decision. Nevertheless, you must not be deceived by the philosophies of the world when it comes to this choice. The Proclamation assists you in determining truth from error. Remember, marriage between a man and a woman is ordained of God. Therefore, as you ponder, pray, keep your covenants, and seek counsel from those you trust, Heavenly Father will guide you with His Spirit. I have a personal testimony of the blessings that can come when you marry in the right place and with the right person.

Questions for Thought and Discussion

1. Why do you want to marry? If you do not want to, why not?

2. What is your vision of a happy, successful marriage?

3. One of the most important commitments you will make in this life is to keep your covenants so that you qualify to go to the temple with the companion of your choice, who also keeps his or her covenants. What are you doing to keep your covenants in spite of the temptations that surround you?

4. How do you feel about only dating those with high standards?

5. Take a blank piece of paper and draw three columns. In the middle column, write "The Proclamation," and list some of the basic principles of the Proclamation. In the first column, write "Mortal Perspective" and in the third column, write "Eternal Perspective." Here is an example:

Mortal Perspective	The Proclamation	Eternal Perspective
Marriage ends with death.	Marriage is ordained by God.	Marriage can endure forever.
Is between any two consenting adults.	Between a man and a woman.	Between a man and a woman.

Suggested Reading

Boyd K. Packer, "For Time and All Eternity," *Ensign*, Nov. 1993.
Dallin H. Oaks, "Divorce," *Ensign*, May 2007.

Chapter 4
Understanding His Plan

Paragraph 1: The family is central to the Creator's plan for the eternal destiny of His children.

Introduction

Elder David Bednar referred to the above sentence in the Proclamation as the "keynote sentence of the Proclamation" because it "teaches us much about the doctrinal significance of marriage and emphasizes the primacy of marriage and family in the Father's plan. . . . *The eternal nature and importance of marriage can be fully understood only within the overarching context of the Father's plan for His children*"[1] (italics added).

One of the reasons people are so confused about marriage and family is they do not understanding that God has a plan for us. Before I became a member of the Church, I had no concept of how important the family was. But when the gospel came into my life, I learned that my future family would be central to God's plan for us, His children.

Our Heavenly Father's Plan: An Eternal Perspective

Perhaps one of the reasons those not affiliated with the Church do not know God has a plan for us is that the word *plan* is not in the Bible. However, it is found thirty-five times in the Book of Mormon and is referred to as the plan of salvation, the plan of happiness, the plan of redemption, and the plan of our God. President Hugh B. Brown, former member of the First Presidency, explained why the family is central to God's plan:

The family concept is one of the major and most important of the whole theological doctrine. In fact, our very concept of heaven itself is the projection of the home into eternity. Salvation, then, is essentially a family affair, and full participation in the plan of salvation can be had only in family units.[2]

A Three-Act Play

Elder Neal A. Maxwell, former member of the Quorum of the Twelve, compared the Father's Plan to a three-act play and taught that certain questions in life can only be understood by the plan of salvation.

Without the Restoration's light on the plan of salvation, trying to comprehend this life is like trying to understand a three-act play while seeing only the second act. Without knowing beginnings and endings, the middle becomes muddled. What is really going on? Is there a director who will make sense of it all? Does the plot have purpose? Such questions are answered only by revelation.[3]

Act 1: Our Pre-Earth Life: The plan of salvation teaches that we lived with heavenly parents as spirit children before we came to this earth. President Brigham Young explained that we are literally children of God.

Things were first created spiritually; the Father actually begat the spirits, and they were brought forth and lived with Him. . . . I want to tell you, each and every one of you, that you are well acquainted with God our Heavenly Father, or the great Eloheim. You are all well acquainted with Him, for there is not a soul of you but what has lived in His house and dwelt with Him year after year; and yet you are seeking to become acquainted with Him, when the fact is, you have merely forgotten what you did know. . . . There is not a person here today but what is a son or daughter of that Being. In the spirit world their spirits were first begotten and brought forth, and they lived there with their parents for ages before they came here. . . . We are the sons and daughters of celestial Beings, and the germ of Deity dwells within us.[4]

Councils were held and God's plan of salvation was presented to us. It was the Prophet Joseph Smith who gave us this understanding: "[We] saw the Savior chosen and appointed and the plan of salvation made, and we sanctioned it."[5] The central purpose of His plan was that we might become like Him and one day return to His presence as families. Again, the Prophet Joseph Smith taught, "God himself, finding He was in the midst of spirits and glory, because He was more intelligent, saw proper to institute laws whereby the rest [His spirit children] could have the privilege to advance like Himself."[6]

For this reason His plan necessitated our being sent to this earth to receive a physical body and gain experience through the use of our moral agency. Agency would result in our choosing to follow His plan or choosing to follow our own will, thus allowing for sin, which would inevitably cause us to fall short. This plan required a Redeemer, someone who would live a perfect life, thus enabling Him to satisfy the demands of God's justice. Jesus Christ, our Father's firstborn spirit son, said He would be our Redeemer and atone for our sins and mistakes. Lucifer objected to the Father's plan and offered to be our savior on the condition that he be given God's power. Satan's idea was rejected and he rebelled against God along with a third of God's spirit offspring. The Prophet Joseph Smith taught that "the contention in heaven was: Jesus said there would be certain souls that would not be saved; and the devil said he could save them all . . ."[7]

Act 2: Mortality: Perhaps some of your friends or acquaintances look at life without knowledge of the first act of life's play. They therefore lack the perspective of why we are here on earth and the importance of marriage and family. The Proclamation states, in paragraph 3, that each of us born on this earth accepted God's plan before we came here, but we have a veil of forgetfulness. The only way we know about our premortal life is through the Restoration of the gospel. The Prophet Joseph Smith explained, "We came to this earth that we might have a body and present it pure before God in the celestial kingdom. The great principle of happiness consists in having a body."[8]

However, once here we likely find that it is not as easy as we thought. Having a physical body and exercising our agency often results in our experiencing pain, sorrow, and disappointment. So to assist us, the Lord has revealed through prophets the plan of happiness. Joseph Smith said, "Happiness is the object and design of our existence; and will be the end thereof, if we pursue the path that leads to it; and this path is virtue, uprightness, faithfulness, holiness, and keeping all the commandments of God."[9]

Central to God's plan was that we should be born into a family where we could be nurtured, taught, and raised in a loving environment. The family thus is essential to His plan for our happiness. Elder Dallin H. Oaks said, "Satan's most strenuous opposition is directed at whatever is most important to the Father's plan. Satan seeks to discredit the Savior and divine authority, to nullify the effects of the Atonement, to counterfeit revelation, to lead people away from the truth, to contradict individual accountability, to confuse gender, to undermine marriage, and to discourage childbearing (especially by parents who will raise children in righteousness).[10]

The family unit is necessary for our happiness and also protection. As said by President Ezra Taft Benson, "Remember, the family is one of God's greatest fortresses against the evils of our day."[11]

Act 3: Life after Death: Through the Prophet Joseph Smith, the Lord restored the truth about life after death and challenged the traditional teachings of Christianity. The Prophet learned that after death we do not immediately go to heaven or hell, but our spirits go to a place called the spirit world where we have the opportunity for continued learning, repenting, and preparing for the final resurrection and judgment. Then, after an allotted time in the spirit world, we are resurrected with an immortal body. (See D&C 88:28.) We will all stand before God to be judged as to whether we qualify to live with Him and our families forever.

Conclusion

Can you see why it is so important to marry someone who believes as you do? Those who marry knowing that what they are doing is part of God's plan have a greater chance of a successful marriage.

Questions for Thought and Discussion

1. You can fill in the blank in the following sentence with any of the evils the devil uses to destroy marriage and family: "How would _____ affect Heavenly Father's plan?"

2. How does the doctrine that God has a plan for you affect your choices here in mortality, especially in regards to your family and loved ones?

Suggested Reading

Dallin H. Oaks, "The Great Plan of Happiness," *Ensign*, Nov. 1993.

Chapter 5
Coming to Know Yourself

Paragraph 2: All human beings—male and female—are created in the image of God. Each is a beloved spirit son or daughter of heavenly parents, and, as such, each has a divine nature and destiny. Gender is an essential characteristic of individual premortal, mortal, and eternal identity and purpose.

Introduction

So it might surprise you to know that one of the most important qualities you take into marriage is your personal feelings of self-worth; not what others think of you, but a conviction of who you really are.

One of the prevalent deceptions in our day is the origin of man. Many of us have been taught in school that we are descended from primates, from ape-like animals, and that man by nature is depraved and base. Confusion also reigns over our gender and why we are male or female. Each of these issues can leave people wondering who they are and why they are here. The Proclamation affirms our individual worth with these doctrines:

- We are each the spirit children of heavenly parents created in their image.

- Because of our divine nature, we have a divine destiny.

- Our gender, determined in premortality, gives each of us an individual and eternal identity.

We Are Spirit Children of Heavenly Parents

In Genesis, the Lord says, "Let us make man in our own image, after our likeness. . . . So God created man in His own image, in the image of God created He him; male and female created He them (Genesis 1:26–27). Elder Boyd K. Packer explained, "No greater ideal has been revealed than the supernal truth that we are children of God, and we differ, by virtue of our creation, from all other living things. . . . No idea has been more *destructive* of happiness . . . no idea has done more to destroy the family than the idea that we are not offspring of God, only advanced animals, compelled to yield to every carnal urge."[1]

Note how this doctrine in the Proclamation can strengthen feelings of self-worth. You are "a beloved spirit son or daughter of heavenly parents" with a "divine nature." The Proclamation does not place any conditions upon your worth to God. It does not say that you are beloved if you are popular, wealthy, handsome, or born into a traditional Latter-day Saint family. You are beloved because of who you were before you ever came here—a son or a daughter of heavenly parents. The Spirit of God can testify to you that this is true.

I had a man come up to me at one point who said, "I have sung 'I am a child of God' all my life, but I have never believed it." This is a doctrine that is important to not just sing about, but actively believe! The fact that we are children of God is the foundation of our feelings of self-worth, which guides our thoughts and actions. People who have positive feelings of self-worth based on an understanding of their divine nature "are more likely to be unselfish, considerate of others, and supportive."[2] Those with negative self-worth tend to be more negative about life and focus on their own wants and needs. They also tend to seek the approval of others, sometimes at the expense of their own values. Perhaps you have known people who sought the approval of others by having sexual relations before marriage, or drinking and partying with friends when, in fact, just the opposite was true: "Wickedness never was happiness" (Alma 41:10). When you keep the Lord's commandments, people respect you and you feel good about who you are. Your Heavenly Father wants you to know that you are His child, that He loves you and He wants you to be happy now and in eternity. Elder George Q. Cannon, former member of the First Presidency, wrote,

Now this is the truth. We humble people, we who feel ourselves sometimes so worthless, so good-for-nothing, we are not so worthless as we think. There is not one of us but what God's love has been expended upon. There is not one of us that He has not cared for and caressed. There is not one of us that He has not desired to save and that He has not devised means to save. There is not one of us that He has not given His angels charge concerning. We may be insignificant and contemptible in our own eyes and in the eyes of others, but the truth remains that we are children of God and that He has actually given His angels . . . charge concerning us, and they watch over us and have us in their keeping.[3]

A Divine Definition of Who We Are

I have a colleague who received a true perspective of his divine nature. He had received his mission call and realized that he had never told God how much he loved Him. So one evening he knelt by a tree in his backyard and poured out his heart in prayer. He told me, "As I knelt there, a voice or feeling came into my mind that said, 'And I love you; you are my son.'" He told me that after that experience people could have said harsh, degrading things to him to put him down, but he stood tall, always assured of his divine nature and potential.

Elder Boyd K. Packer said, "You are a child of God. He is the father of your spirit. Spiritually you are of noble birth, the offspring of the King of Heaven. Fix that truth in your mind and hold to it. However many generations in your mortal ancestry, no matter what race or people you represent, the pedigree of your spirit can be written on a single line. You are a child of God."[4]

Satan Tried to Steal Moses's True Identity

One of the clearest examples of how Satan tries to destroy our divine identity is found in the first chapter of Moses in the Pearl of Great Price. In a glorious vision that Moses had of the premortal Savior, he was told, "Behold, I am the Lord God Almighty. . . . And behold, *thou art my son*. . . . And I have a work for thee, Moses, *my son*" (Moses 1:3–6; italics added). Here, it was Jesus Christ speaking for the Father, so it was God that taught Moses his true identity through the medium of the Savior.

Following this vision, Satan came to Moses and said, "Moses, *son of man*, worship me" (Moses 1:12; italics added). Because Moses had a divine definition of his true identity, he was able to say to Satan, "Who art thou? For behold, *I am a son of God* in the similitude of His Only Begotten" (Moses 1:13; italics added).

Satan Is Seeking to Destroy Your True Identity

If you succumb to the adversary's deceptions, you could make some potentially fatal mistakes. You need to remember constantly who you are and your divine purpose here on earth. The following are some ways the devil may seek to steal away your true identity:

- Negative thoughts may come into your mind such as being worthless, stupid, or unattractive.

- You may feel that you are unworthy to pray or attend church.

- You may be overly obsessive about your physical appearance.

- You may have negative thoughts about yourself because you do not date a lot.

You have probably experienced some of these feelings at various times in your life. At these moments, Satan attempts to steal your identity, replacing it with a lesser, negative form.

I remember hearing a story that the devil had a garage sale where he displayed all of his tools of temptation, each having a price attached. A person asked him why one of his tools was priced so much higher than the others. He replied, "Because with that tool I can get people to do almost anything I want." That tool was discouragement.

When we are depressed, discouraged, or upset, what can we do? President Monson has offered these suggestions;

> To live greatly, we must develop the capacity to face trouble with courage, disappointment with cheerfulness, and triumph with humility. You ask, "How might we achieve these goals?" I answer, "By getting a true perspective of who you really are!" We are sons and daughters of a living God in whose image we have been created.[5]

When we remember who we really are, we can receive strength to press forward with faith in Heavenly Father and the Savior.

President Gordon B. Hinckley elaborates, "I believe that I am a child of God endowed with a divine birthright. I believe that there is something of divinity within me and within each of you. I believe that we have a godly inheritance and that it is our responsibility, our obligation, and our opportunity to cultivate and nurture the very best of those qualities within us."[6]

The Importance of a Patriarchal Blessing

One of the blessings Heavenly Father has given to worthy members of the Church is a patriarchal blessing. This blessing, given from Him through a stake patriarch, can help you understand who you really are and your divine potential. It has two purposes: first, it declares your lineage, to which tribe, or family, in the house of Israel you belong. This is important because a declaration of lineage gives you the opportunity to receive the blessings and responsibilities of the Abrahamic Covenant. These blessings include the promise of an eternal marriage and family based on your keeping the covenants made in the temple. The responsibilities include sharing the gospel with others and being an example of Jesus Christ. Second, it provides information to guide you. Your blessing will likely contain promises, admonitions, and warnings. President Monson described a patriarchal blessing as a "personal Liahona to chart your course and guide your way."[7]

I had an experience that taught me how a patriarchal blessing can benefit our lives. When I was teaching institute, I met a young man who had a very interesting story. He told me that as a young boy he was heavyset and short. Kids at school made fun of him and called him "stubby chubby." Sometimes after school, kids would take a rope, tie him to a tree, and leave him until his single mom got home from work and came looking for him. To say the least, he did not have positive feelings of self-worth. He told me that he got so discouraged and depressed that he had tried to commit suicide twice. He was about to try a third time, but before doing so, he went to his dresser and opened a drawer, looking for something. His fingers touched some pieces of paper. He pulled them out and discovered they were his patriarchal blessing. He sat down and read them. He told me it changed his perspective on himself and on life. He discovered that God loved him and he had a purpose in life.

Gender Gives Us an Individual and Eternal Identity

Have you ever wondered how gender was determined? Was it simply by chance or because of DNA? The Proclamation teaches that before you were born into mortality, you were male or female. The spirit within your physical body was a son or daughter of God before you ever came here, and you will be such throughout eternity. Why you were chosen, assigned, or designated to be male or female we do not know, but Elder Boyd K. Packer has taught that at our spirit birth we were male or female.

> As we learn about ourselves and learn about the great plan of redemption, we know that in the premortal existence intelligence existed forever. It was not created. It will exist forever. In due course, we were given a spirit body. We became then the sons and daughters of God. We had gender then. We were male or female.[8]

The Proclamation does state that your gender has purpose. The fact that you are male or female helps you understand the particular gifts that God has given you. It also helps you understand the complementary roles man and woman have in marriage. Elder Dallin H. Oaks taught why our gender is essential to our Heavenly Father's plan.

> Maleness and femaleness, marriage, and the bearing and nurturing of children are all essential to the great plan of happiness. Modern revelation makes clear that what we call gender was part of our existence prior to our birth. God declares that he created "male and female" (D&C 20:18; Moses 2:7; Genesis 1:27). Elder James E. Talmage explained: "The distinction between male and female is no condition peculiar to the relatively brief period of mortal life; it was an essential characteristic of our pre-existent condition (*Millennial Star*, August 1922, 539). . . . There are many political, legal, and social pressures for changes that confuse gender and homogenize the difference between men and women. Our eternal perspective sets us against changes that alter those separate duties and privileges of men and women that are essential to accomplish the great plan of happiness.[9]

Conclusion

Reflect for a few minutes on what Heavenly Father has provided for you in this paragraph of the Proclamation:

- *You have a divine nature*; you are a child of God.

- *You have a divine destiny*; because you are His son or daughter, you have divinity within you and a purpose for being on earth.

- *You have been given a divine plan*; The gospel gives you a chartered course as to how you can achieve your divine destiny to live with Heavenly Father and your family forever.

Divine nature. Divine Plan. Divine destiny. Can you sense how much the Lord cares about you and how much He loves you? Because you are a child of God, you are an heir to eternal life—God's life. His life is centered in the family and His divine plan enables you to have your family forever.

Questions for Thought and Discussion

1. Do you really believe you are a child of God?

2. How could the doctrine that you have a divine nature and destiny affect your daily decisions?

3. Do you read your patriarchal blessing regularly, looking for special counsel, warnings, or promises the Lord has given you? If you do not have a patriarchal blessing, consider talking with your bishop about receiving one.

4. What special gifts has Heavenly Father given you because of your gender?

Suggested Reading

Richard G. Scott, "Healing the Tragic Scars of Abuse," *Ensign*, May 1992, 49.

Dallin H. Oaks, "Same-Gender Attraction," *Ensign*, October, 1995.

Chapter 6
You Have a Purpose Here

Paragraph 3: In the premortal realm, spirit sons and daughters knew and worshipped God as their Eternal Father and accepted His plan by which His children could obtain a physical body and gain earthly experience to progress toward perfection and ultimately realize their divine destiny as heirs of eternal life.

Introduction

We do not know much about our premortal life because of the veil that has been placed over our memory. The Proclamation says that we knew our Heavenly Father and worshipped Him there. It further teaches that we accepted His plan to come to this earth and experience mortality. I had a woman say to me that she had so many problems she didn't know what to do. I reminded her that she voted for this before she came here. She looked at me and said, "Let me vote again!" Have you ever felt like that?

Four Purposes for Our Mortal Experience

This paragraph of the Proclamation explains clearly why we are here on earth and what our ultimate purpose and destiny are.

- To receive a physical body.

- To gain earthly experience.

- To progress toward perfection.

- To become heirs of eternal life.

We Looked Forward to Receiving a Body

I have talked with some people who feel that their physical body is a step down in their progression. In reality, our body is a step up in our progression as we seek to become like our Heavenly Father, who has a glorified, immortal body.

Elder Douglas Callister, former member of the Seventy, said that in premortal life we looked forward to receiving a physical body. "Indeed a gift for which you may have prayed a thousand times, ten thousand times before you entered mortality."[1]

In President Joseph F. Smith's vision of life after death in the spirit world, he noted that the people longed to have their physical body. "For the dead had looked upon the long absence of their spirits from their bodies as bondage" (D&C 138:50).

Much of the happiness we receive here in mortality is because of our physical body: the ability to taste foods, to smell flowers, to hold hands with our sweetheart, to hear beautiful music, and to see a magnificent sunset. Too often we take the gift of the body for granted until we lose the ability to do something.

Our body can also be a source of pain and unhappiness. Addictions to things such as alcohol and drugs can have a powerful negative effect on us. Misuse of our physical body is a sin. Paul warned us that God will hold us accountable for how we treat our body. "Know ye not that ye are the temple of God, and that the Spirit of God dwelleth in you? If any man defile the temple of God, him shall God destroy; for the temple of God is holy, which temple ye are" (I Corinthians 3:16–17).

You probably realize that most people do not share our belief about the sanctity of our physical body. The people you choose to date, especially if they are not committed Latter-day Saints or those with similar values, will have different standards regarding physical relationships. Let me illustrate what I mean:

Committed Latter-day Saints	Those Not Committed to Church Standards
My physical body is a gift from God and I must take care of it.	My body is my own and there to give me pleasure.
Sexual relations are reserved for a married man and woman.	If a couple loves each other, then it is okay to have sexual relations.

So you must choose carefully the people you date and associate with. It makes your life and choices easier, now as well as in the future.

Why Do We Need Our Physical Body?

The Prophet Joseph Smith taught, "We came to this earth that we might have a body and present it pure before God in the celestial kingdom. The great principle of happiness consists in having a body. The devil has no body, and herein is his punishment. He is pleased when he can obtain the tabernacle of man. . . . All beings who have bodies have power over those who have not."[2]

Because Satan will never have a physical body, he tempts you relentlessly to give him control of your body. You can actually lose your will and your ability to choose if you do not heed the counsel of prophets and apostles. One of the most significant ways we lose our agency, as indicated above, is through addictions. Much heartache and many problems have been caused by people addicted to pornography, sex, shopping, alcohol, tobacco, gambling, illegal drugs, and so on. Elder Douglas Callister said,

> Satan intends to destroy your spirit through your body. He makes worldly enticements all look so attractive. Nevertheless, you may be certain who is the author of inducements to look at pornography, live immorally, experiment with improper substances, and violate, mark, expose, defile, or neglect your body. And that author is not your friend.[3]

Our physical body—if treated well—gives us power over the devil and his temptations. When we give in to his temptations, we give him power over us. I have known a number of young people who thought they knew more than the prophets and apostles. They believed at eighteen or twenty they could do what they wanted: drink alcohol, take illegal drugs, have sexual relations before marriage. If we were to follow their lives, we would find much regret and many consequences that have undoubtedly lessened their happiness.

We Came to Earth to Gain Experience

Our Heavenly Father has given us the priceless gift of agency, the ability to make choices. But with agency comes consequences. We gain experience and maturity by learning to recognize consequences.

Learning by experience is often very painful but it is etched into our souls and is not forgotten all that easily. One of the signs of maturity is when we actually consider the consequences before we make the choice. Satan would have us think only of the moment and forget about the possible results. In fact, that was his idea in premortality: to send us to earth where we could do whatever we wanted with no consequences. No wonder that idea had many followers.

I recall reading the story of a young man who worked for a company that had just hired a new manager in his department. He thought he might take the opportunity to visit with her to see what suggestions she might have for him so he could progress in the company. He asked her, "What is your formula for success?" She replied, "Make right decisions." He asked, "How do I learn to do that?" "Experience," she said. "Experience." "But how do I gain experience?" She looked him straight in the eye and said, "Bad decisions." Sadly enough, she is probably right. But the Lord is not happy when we make the same bad decisions over and over again. He wants us to learn from our experiences. Look back on your life. What decisions would you change had you considered the possible consequences?

We Came Here to Progress Toward Perfection

Perfection—becoming like Heavenly Father and Christ—is a lifelong process that will not end when we die. Joseph Smith taught,

> When you climb up a ladder, you must begin at the bottom, and ascend step by step, until you arrive at the top; and so it is with the principles of the gospel—you must begin with the first, and go on until you learn all the principles of exaltation. But it will be a great while after you have passed through the veil before you will have learned them. It is not all to be comprehended in this world; it will be a great work to learn our salvation and exaltation even beyond the grave.[4]

Perfection is made possible because of the Atonement of Jesus Christ, who offers us the supernal gift of repentance. Our sins, as Alma taught, may be blotted out "according to the power of His deliverance" (Alma 7:13). The Lord has promised, "Behold, he who has repented of his sins, the same is forgiven, and I, the Lord, remember them no more" (D&C 58:42).

Perfection is achieved one small step at a time, as we strive to become more like our Savior. Though, as King Benjamin taught, it is not our works that save us; our works only qualify us for His grace, which enables us to receive heavenly help to overcome our weaknesses. Marriage and family are a great help with our efforts to acquire the attributes of Jesus Christ, for it is in the family that we learn patience, love, and forgiveness. The family then becomes our apprenticeship for eternal life.

The doctrine of becoming perfect has two sides. On one side, it can be a constant motivating factor to do and be our best. And on the other side, it can be used by the devil to discourage and depress us. Have you ever felt, "I'll never make it. It is just too hard"? This is certainly not the Lord speaking to us. Remember Alma teaching his son Corianton about the Atonement of Jesus Christ and repentance? Corianton had been immoral during his mission to the Zoramites.

His father taught him that because of the mercy of God, he could repent and be forgiven. Then he told Corianton, "And now, my son, I desire that ye should let these things [his former sins] trouble you no more, and only let your sins [now] trouble you, with that trouble which shall bring you down to repentance" (Alma 42: 29).

I took this to mean that Alma was saying something like, "You have now repented of that sin so don't constantly beat on yourself with it. Worry now about sins yet to come in your life and prepare to repent of them."

Elder Boyd K. Packer taught the following:

> Some worry endlessly over missions that were missed, or marriages that did not turn out, or babies that did not arrive, or children that seem lost, or dreams unfulfilled, or because age limits what they can do. I do not think it pleases the Lord when we worry because we think we never do enough or that what we do is never good enough. Some needlessly carry a heavy burden of guilt which could be removed through . . . repentance.[5]

Pierre Teilhard de Chardin said, "We are not human beings having a spiritual experience. We are spiritual beings having a human experience."[6]

Our Ultimate Goal Is to Be Heirs of Eternal Life

When Susan went to the hospital to give birth to our first child, I was asked to wait in the "heirport." An *heir* is one who receives an inheritance from a family member or someone else, which can be money, property, or other valuables. In the case of me waiting in an "heirport," Susan was giving birth to a child who would become our "heir."

Abinadi, in the Book of Mormon, taught the people of King Noah that those who hearkened unto the words of the prophets and believed in the redemption of Christ would become "heirs to the kingdom of God." (See Mosiah 15:11.) The most valuable inheritance we can receive is from Heavenly Father, who offers us the type of life He has: eternal life. To become an heir of God's life, we must follow the path He has outlined for us. But this raises the question of what eternal life or exaltation in the highest degree of the celestial kingdom is like? President Lorenzo Snow gave us this description of exaltation:

> Our travel in this path of exaltation will bring us to the fullness of our Lord Jesus Christ, to stand in the presence of our Father, to receive of His fullness, to have the pleasure of increasing in our posterity worlds without end, to enjoy those pleasant association that we have had in this life, to have our sons and our daughters, our husbands and our wives, surrounded with all the enjoyment that heaven can bestow, our bodies glorified like unto the Savior's, . . . free from the disappointments and vexations and the unpleasant sacrifices that we are making here.[7]

Perhaps those weeping and wailing and gnashing their teeth spoken of in the scriptures are those who had the gospel but chose to live the ways of the world.

Conclusion

By treating our physical body as a temple, choosing to use our agency to be obedient to the Lord, and striving to become like Heavenly Father and Christ, we may one day receive an immortal, celestial body. One of the tests of mortality, particularly during dating, is learning to control the desires of our flesh. And, as said by Elder F. Burton Howard, "If you want something to last forever, you treat it differently. You shield it and protect it. You never abuse it."[8]

Questions for Thought and Discussion

1. Read each verse in Hymn 292, "O My Father." What does this hymn teach you about our heavenly parents?

2. What are some of the things you can do to protect your physical body?

3. Read carefully the promises given to those who obey the Word of Wisdom. (See D&C 89:18–21.) How are these promises useful in your life?

4. As you look back on your life, what experiences have you had that will help you make better decisions now and in the future?

5. Have you decided to remember Jesus Christ everyday of your life? What can you do to always remember Him?

Suggested Reading

N. Eldon Tanner, "The Eternal Nature of Marriage," *Ensign*, May, 2011.

Quinton L. Cook, "The Doctrine of the Father," *Ensign*, Feb. 2010.

Chapter 7
Committed to the Temple

Paragraph 3: The divine plan of happiness enables family relationships to be perpetuated beyond the grave. Sacred ordinances and covenants available in holy temples make it possible for individuals to return to the presence of God and for families to be united eternally.

Introduction

The day Susan and I were married in the Salt Lake Temple is unforgettable. We were married on Friday the thirteenth so if the marriage didn't work out, we could blame it on the day. (Just kidding.) When Susan and I knelt at the altar of the temple, Elder LeGrand Richards, a former member of the Quorum of the Twelve Apostles, was the officiator. After he had pronounced us husband and wife, he looked at me and said, "Brother McIntosh, do you know how long you will be able to live with this beautiful daughter of God, if you are worthy?" I responded, "Forever." He looked at me and said, "Can you really conceive of forever? I like to think in terms of a number I can understand. If you are worthy, you will be able to live with Susan for 300 million years. I like to round it off to the nearest millionth." I thought, *Wow! What a wonderful thing. I get to live with Susan (if I am worthy) for 300 million years.*

What Is a Temple?

In the church we say the temple is the House of the Lord. It is also seven houses within one glorious house. The Lord has said,

"Organize yourselves; prepare every needful thing; and establish a house [temple], even a house of prayer, a house of fasting, a house of faith, a house of learning, a house of glory, a house of order, a house of God" (D&C 88:119). Let's look at each of these seven houses.

- A house of prayer. The temple is a place where we can pray and seek answers to the challenges we face in life.

- A house of fasting. When attending the temple and seeking special blessings, fasting can increase our closeness to the Lord.

- A house of faith. The ordinances we experience in the temple can strengthen our faith and deepen our love for the Lord.

- A house of learning. The temple has been referred to as the "university of the Lord." In the temple we learn to know the Lord, what He desires of us, and what His hopes are for us. We also learn of ourselves, whom we really are, and what our divine potential is.

- A house of glory. Indeed, the glory of God is intelligence, or light and truth (D&C 93:36). Temples are filled with the light of the Spirit. We feel of God's presence and that warms our souls and brings us peace.

- A house of order. Through the temple ordinances, we put our lives in the proper order that God has prescribed for us to attain eternal life. By keeping the covenants associated with these ordinances, we become sanctified by His Spirit.

- A house of God. President Harold B. Lee was once asked where the Lord had appeared in a particular temple. He replied, "This is the most likely place he would come when he comes on earth. Don't ask for a certain place because he has walked these halls."[1]

What Do We Mean When We Say Temple Marriage?

One of the best answers I have found to this question was given by former apostle Elder Bruce R. McConkie.

When we as Latter-day Saints talk about marriage we are talking about a holy celestial order. We are talking about a system out of which can grow the greatest love, joy, peace, happiness, and serenity known to humankind. We are talking about creating a family unit that has the potential of being everlasting and eternal, a family unit where a man and a wife can go on in that relationship to all eternity, and where mother and daughter and father and son are bound by eternal ties that will never be severed.[2]

Notice that Elder McConkie used the words *can* grow and has the *potential* of being everlasting and eternal. I believe that Elder McConkie is alluding to the fact that there is a difference between a temple marriage and a celestial marriage. John Bytheway illustrated this clearly when he said, "A 'temple marriage' indicates a *location*, but a 'celestial marriage' indicates a *quality*"[3] (italics added).

Certainly many temple marriages are not celestial marriages. But all celestial marriages must begin with a temple marriage. This chapter will focus on why a temple marriage is so important and how you can prepare for a celestial marriage.

Eternal Marriage Was Revealed to Joseph Smith

When Parley P. Pratt, a member of the original Quorum of the Twelve Apostles, heard for the first time the doctrine of eternal marriage from the Prophet Joseph Smith, he said,

It was Joseph Smith who taught me how to prize the endearing relationships of father and mother, husband and wife; of brother and sister, son and daughter. It was from him that I learned that the wife of my bosom might be secured to me for time and eternity; and that the refined sympathies and affections which endeared us to each other emanated from the fountain of divine eternal love. . . . I had loved before, but I knew not why. But now I loved—with a pureness—an intensity of elevated, exalted feeling, which would lift my soul from these transitory things of this grovelling sphere and expand it as the ocean.[4]

Today we look to the Prophet Joseph Smith as the one the Lord had restore the blessings of temple work. Temples are an evidence of God's love for His children, for it is only in temples that husbands and wives and children can receive the promise of being eternally together. The Proclamation states, "Sacred ordinances and covenants available in holy temples make it possible for individuals to return to the presence of God and for families to be united eternally."

Ordinances Make a Celestial Marriage Possible

I must admit my first experience going to the temple was quite frustrating. What I loved about the Church when I first went to a meeting was the simplicity and lack of formalism. You might say I disliked ritual and symbolism. The problem when I received my own endowment was I was not prepared. Some years later, I came to realize that God loves using symbols, and as Elder Orson F. Whitney said, "It is His favorite method of teaching."[5] We see this so clearly in the Old Testament and the New Testament with Christ's parables and the Book of Revelation. When we understand that God uses symbols to teach truth to those who are spiritually prepared and to conceal truth from those not prepared, the ordinances of the gospel begin to take on greater meaning.

You have probably heard the terms *traffic ordinances* or *city ordinances*. Ordinances like these are governmental laws or regulations. When used in a gospel context, ordinances are laws ordained by God that have at least three characteristics:

1. Those who have priesthood authority administer each gospel ordinance. It was necessary for the priesthood to be restored to the earth for ordinances to be performed and to be valid.

2. Ordinances are physical acts that are symbolic of a spiritual truth. In Doctrine and Covenants section 29:34, the Lord says, "All things unto me are spiritual, and not at any time have I given unto you a law which was temporal." For example, baptism is symbolic of being born again to a new life with Christ. Kneeling at an altar during a temple marriage is symbolic of inviting Jesus Christ into the marriage and willingness to sacrifice for each other as He sacrificed His life.

3. Ordinances also involve covenants between us and Heavenly Father. The covenants are what create a celestial marriage. As we keep our covenants with the Lord, we are blessed with power from on high to resist evil and are protected from the

deceptions of the devil. Referring to the importance of the ordinances of the temple, the Lord taught the early saints, "Yea, verily I say unto you, I gave unto you a commandment that you should build a house, in the which house I design to endow those whom I have chosen with power from on high" (D&C 95:8).

The Covenant Path Back to God

The road back to our Father in Heaven is found in the ordinances of the restored gospel. The Prophet Joseph Smith taught that the ordinances that are required for eternal life were established before we ever came to this earth.[6]

There are five essential ordinances that are necessary for eternal life, and each involves covenants we make with God. Two of these ordinances can only be done in temples. You might think of each of these ordinances as steps along a path back to Heavenly Father.

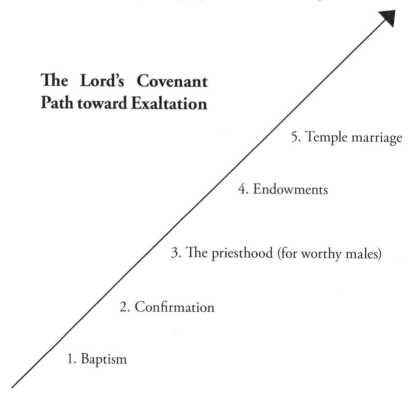

The Lord's Covenant Path toward Exaltation

5. Temple marriage

4. Endowments

3. The priesthood (for worthy males)

2. Confirmation

1. Baptism

Look carefully at these steps. Which ones have you already taken? What steps are ahead of you as you seek to create your own eternal marriage and family? The best way to prepare for the next step is to keep the covenants you have already made in previous steps.

Elijah Restored the Sealing Power of Marriage

Malachi, the last Old Testament prophet, prophesied, "Behold, I will send you Elijah the prophet before the coming of the great and dreadful day of the Lord: And he shall turn the heart of the fathers to the children, and the heart of the children to their fathers, lest I come and smite the earth with a curse" (Malachi 4:5–6).

President Joseph Fielding Smith referred to the keys that Elijah restored as the crowning blessing of the restoration, "the authority to seal both on earth and in heaven, husbands and wives and children to parents."[7]

On April 3, 1836, Moses, Elias, and Elijah appeared in the Kirtland Temple to the Prophet Joseph Smith and Oliver Cowdery. (See D&C 110.) Moses committed to them the keys of the gathering of Israel (missionary work). Elias committed to them the keys of the dispensation of Abraham whereby we can be organized into eternal families. Elijah restored the sealing power by which all gospel ordinances—performed by the priesthood on earth—are bound in heaven. Suppose for just a moment that Elijah never appeared. What would that mean to you? Could families be together forever?

President Henry B. Eyring taught,

> It is important to know why the Lord promised to send Elijah. Elijah was a great prophet with great power given him by God. He held the greatest power God gives to His children: he held the sealing power, the power to bind on earth and have it bound in heaven. . . . And the Lord kept His promise to send Elijah.[8]

The keys to seal husband and wife and parents to children are on the earth today and the only place where we can access these keys is in a temple.

President Brigham Young believed that it was worth every effort to marry in the Lord's way (and remember, airplanes did not exist in the his day):

> There is not a young man in our community who would not be willing to travel from here to England to be married right, if he

understood things as they are; there is not a young woman in our community, who loves the Gospel and wishes its blessings, that would be married in any other way [than in the temple of God].[9]

Live Worthily to Receive a Temple Recommend

A plaque on the front of the Cardston Alberta Temple contains these words, written by Elder Orson F. Whitney:

> Hearts must be pure to come within these walls,
> Where lies a feast unknown to festive halls.
> Freely partake, for freely God hath giv'n,
> And taste the holy joys that tell of heav'n.
> Here learn of Him who triumphed o'er the grave,
> And unto men the keys, the kingdom gave.
> Joined here by pow'rs that past and present bind,
> The living and the dead perfection find.

Some have asked the question, "Why do we need to have an interview to enter the temple?" The answer, "The temple is God's house and He decides who may enter." Here are some of the gospel principles and commandments that you need to be living to worship in the temple:

1. Do you have a testimony of God the Eternal Father and His Son, Jesus Christ?

2. Do you have a testimony of the restoration of the gospel through the Prophet Joseph Smith?

3. Do you live a morally clean life?

4. Do you live the law of tithing?

5. Do you live the Word of Wisdom?

6. Do you keep the Sabbath day holy?

7. Are you honest with others?

I desire with all of my heart that all would live worthy lives so they could enter into God's holy temple. You might ask why I feel this way. Because in His house, away from the noise and commotion of the world, you can feel love and peace. I heard one young woman bear her testimony and say, "The first time I went to the temple, I felt love." I have asked many people why they go to the temple time after time. Their answer, "In the temple, I feel peace."

How Strong Is Your Desire for Temple Marriage?

Mark and Janice had been dating for a couple of months and felt they loved each other. Mark was not a member of the Church and believed as long as they were in love they could have sexual relations. Janice rejected his advances, telling him that she wanted to be married in the temple. Mark kept insisting and gradually wore Janice down to the point that she gave in to his desires. Her dreams for a temple marriage were shattered. At what point did Janice make the decision that caused her to be unworthy of receiving a temple recommend? If she had come to you for advice before the point that she given in to Mark, what would you have said to her?

Contrast this story with a young woman Susan and I met who has been an example of one who had a strong commitment to marry in the temple. She had been dating a man who was raised in the church but was not active. She told us that he had many wonderful qualities that would make him a good husband; however, he could not take her to the temple. I asked her what happened. She replied, "I broke up with him." I asked, "Wasn't that hard to do?" She responded, "Yes, but I knew what I wanted." Her desire for a temple marriage was stronger than her desire to marry a man who could not take her to the temple. She knew what she wanted. *Have you decided what you want?*

President Gordon B. Hinckley has testified,

> There is no substitute for marrying in the temple. It is the only place under the heavens where marriage can be solemnized for eternity. Don't cheat yourself. Don't cheat your companion. Don't shortchange your lives. . . . Marry the right person in the right place at the right time. . . . Choose a companion of your own faith.[10]

Susan and I faced a big challenge before we were married. My parents were not members of the Church and we considered getting married civilly so they could be at the ceremony. We went to our stake president and shared with him our thoughts. He said, "This is your marriage, so how do *you* want to be married?" We both responded, "In the temple." "Then," he said, "have faith and be married the way the Lord would have you marry." We were married in the temple and that decision has blessed our lives ever since.

Conclusion

Consider the following promise made by Elder Boyd K. Packer:

The Lord will bless us as we attend to the sacred ordinance work of the temples. Blessings there will not be limited to our temple service. We will be blessed in all of our affairs. . . . Our labors in the temple cover us with a shield and a protection, both individually and as a people.[11]

Questions for Thought and Discussion

1. Look up in the Topical Guide of the Bible the following words: endowment, marriage, temples. Study the scripture references for each of the words. What did you take away from your reading?

2. If you haven't been through the temple, have you attended a temple preparation class? Ask your bishop if one is available.

3. Read carefully Doctrine and Covenants 90:24. What promise does the Lord make to you if you remember your covenants?

4. Read Doctrine and Covenants 97:15–16. Why does Satan want to keep you from the temple?

5. If you have already been to the temple, do you have a current temple recommend, and are you using it?

Suggested Reading

Boyd K. Packer, "The Holy Temple", *Ensign*, February 1995, 32.

Carlos E. Asay, "The Temple Garment: An Outward Expression of an Inward Commitment," *Ensign*, August 1997, 18.

Henry B. Eyring, "Families under Covenant," *Ensign*, May 2012.

Russell M. Nelson, "The Spirit of Elijah," *Ensign*, November 1994.

Chapter 8

Is It Love or Lust?

Paragraph 4: We further declare that God has commanded that the sacred powers of procreation are to be employed only between man and woman, lawfully wedded as husband and wife.

Introduction

One of the most serious challenges young people face as they prepare for marriage is distinguishing love from lust. Lust is a strong craving for something such as food, money, or power; however, when related to romance, lust is a strong craving for physical intimacy. Lust can begin as a small burning ember that, when fueled by pornography or immorality, becomes a raging fire.

Elder David A. Bednar spoke concerning this,

> The precise nature of the test of mortality, then, can be summarized in the following question: Will I respond to the inclinations of the natural man, or will I yield to the enticing of the Holy Spirit and become a saint through the Atonement of Christ the Lord (see Mosiah 3:19)? That is the test. Every appetite, desire, propensity, and impulse of the natural man may be overcome by and through the Atonement of Jesus Christ. We are here on the earth to develop godlike qualities and to bridle all of the passions of the flesh.[1]

This Desire within Us Is Good

Apostles and prophets have clearly taught that the attraction and physical desires we have for the opposite sex are good when reserved for marriage. Prophets of the Lord have also taught that in God's plan there are two purposes for procreative powers: to bring God's spirit children into the world and to be a bond of love between a married man and woman.[2] Any other use of this sacred power is strictly forbidden by the Lord.

Love or Lust?

Lust, as we discussed at the beginning of this chapter, is a craving for sexual intimacy. It is selfish, all about a person's appetites and passions. If lust is at one end of a continuum, love is at the other end. Love, as discussed in chapter 11, is a desire to give of yourself to assist and serve others. It is characterized by not wanting do anything that would hurt or injure another person. When a couple begins to become involved in sexual acts before marriage, lust starts to enter into the relationship and love walks out the door.

How Serious Is the Misuse of This Sacred Power?

In the Book of Mormon, Corianton went on a mission to the apostate Zoramites with his father, Alma the Younger. He heard of the beauty of Isabel and her harlot friends, so he left his mission and committed fornication with Isabel. His father later told him that she had stolen away the hearts of many, but that was no excuse for him. Why? Because Corianton had made sacred covenants with the Lord in the ordinances of baptism, confirmation, and receiving the holy priesthood. How serious was his sin? Alma told him it was "an abomination in the sight of the Lord; yea, most abominable above all sins save it be the shedding of innocent blood or denying the Holy Ghost" (Alma 39:5). He then said that immorality is so serious "that it is not easy for him to obtain forgiveness" (Alma 39:6). We know that Corianton repented because he was later called to preach the word of God again (Alma 42:31). However, we have no record of the remorse and suffering he went through before he received forgiveness. Like Corianton, anyone who is immoral must go through the process of repentance to be forgiven.

President Boyd K. Packer has explained that the consequences of immorality are guilt and pain, but the one who has sinned may be forgiven. "Know then, my young friends, that there is a great cleansing power. And know that you can be clean . . . there is a way, not entirely painless, but certainly possible. You can stand clean and spotless before Him. Guilt will be gone, and you can be at peace. Go to your bishop. He holds the key to this cleansing power."[3]

How Does Immorality Affect Dating Couples?

Elder Richard G. Scott of the Quorum of the Twelve Apostles has said that when immorality enters a relationship, it drives the Holy Spirit out.

> One purpose of this private, sacred, intimate experience is to provide the physical bodies for the spirits Father in Heaven wants to experience mortality. Another reason for these powerful and beautiful feelings of love is to bind husband and wife together in loyalty, fidelity, consideration of each other, and common purpose. However, those intimate acts are forbidden by the Lord outside the enduring commitment of marriage because they undermine His purposes. Within the sacred covenant of marriage, such relationships are according to His plan. When experienced any other way, they are against His will. . . . [It] creates a barrier to the influence of the Holy Spirit with all its uplifting, enlightening, and empowering capabilities.[4]

President Ezra Taft Benson has also warned that immorality causes love to wither and die.

> There is no lasting happiness in immorality. . . . There may be momentary pleasure. For a time it may seem like everything is wonderful. But quickly the relationship will sour. . . . Love begins to die. Bitterness, jealousy, anger, and even hate begin to grow. All of these are the natural results of sin and transgression.[5]

How Do You Stay Morally Clean?

First, you have been blessed with an understanding of the plan of happiness, which is a protection to you from the temptations of the devil who wants you to be as miserable as he is (see 2 Nephi 2:27). Elder Boyd K. Packer has referred to the importance of God's plan: "Without knowledge of the gospel plan, transgression seems natural, innocent, even justified. There is no greater protection from the adversary than for us to know the truth—to know the plan."[6]

Second, understand when immorality actually begins. Look at the following list and determine when you think immorality begins.

- Fornication and sexual relations

- Petting (touching the other person's private areas)

- Making out

- Goodnight kiss

- Hugging

- Holding hands

When did you think it begins? Here is what President Spencer W. Kimball, has said,

> Kissing has been prostituted and has been degenerated to develop lust instead of affection, honor, and admiration. What is miscalled the soul kiss [French kissing] is an abomination and stirs passion that results in the eventual loss of virtue. Even if timely courtship justifies a kiss, it should be a clean, decent, sexless one. . . . If the soul kiss with its passion were eliminated from dating, there would be an immediate upswing in chastity, with fewer illegitimate babies, fewer unwed mothers, fewer forced marriages, and fewer unhappy souls.[7]

Passionate kissing can raise sexual desire to a point that a person is almost incapable of saying "no." Anyone who has ever been immoral will probably tell you it began with passionate kissing. It takes great faith in today's dating culture to keep a kiss sacred.

Third, seek to keep your thoughts clean and pure. Speaking about men, two authors wrote, "Men have a visual ignition switch when it comes to viewing the female anatomy."[8] Men, to stay morally clean, must control what they look at. The Lord has said in no uncertain terms the results of lust: "And he that looketh upon a woman to lust after her shall deny the faith, and shall not have the Spirit; and if he repents not he shall be cast out [excommunicated]" (D&C 42:23; see also 63:16).

Part of this mortal test is learning to master the self. President Gordon B. Hinckley said,

> Mental control must be stronger than physical appetites or desires of the flesh. As thoughts are brought into complete harmony with revealed truth, actions will then become appropriate. The timeless proverb is as true now as when it was first spoken: "For as a man thinketh in his heart, so is he" (Proverbs 23:7). Each of us, with

discipline and effort, has the capacity to control his thoughts and actions. This is part of the process of developing spiritual, physical, and emotional maturity.[9]

Fourth, be a true disciple of Jesus Christ. Elder Jeffrey R. Holland has shared this insight as to how you can remain morally clean.

> Do you want capability, safety, and security in dating and romance, in married life and eternity? Be a true disciple of Jesus. Be a genuine, committed, word-and-deed Latter-day Saint. Believe that your faith has everything to do with your romance, because it does. You separate dating from discipleship at your peril. Jesus Christ, the Light of the World, is the only lamp by which you can successfully see the path of love and happiness.[10]

Fifth, follow this counsel by Sister Susan Tanner, former President of the Young Women of the Church, which she shared with the students of BYU–Idaho. Her counsel is good advice for anyone who is single and desires to stay chaste before marriage.

- Avoid the dangers of the dark. Stay in well lighted places, literally and figuratively. There is wisdom to leaving the lights on—on the porch, in the living room, at the dance. And there's safety in shunning places that feel dark in spirit.

- Beware the hazard of the horizontal. Don't lie down together with a date. Just don't do it—not to watch a movie, or to read a book, or to rest at a picnic.

- Remember the perils of privacy. Find public places to be alone. Learn to have your intimate talks where others are. There is great safety in being together where you can be easily interrupted.

- Modesty is a must. Everything about your appearance, your speech, and your demeanor should bespeak that you are a literal spirit son or daughter of Heavenly Father. If we truly understand the paramount significance of our bodies in our Father's plan, we would show great honor for our bodies. When you dress and act modestly, others also will treat you with respect.[11]

What Do You Do If You Have Been Immoral or Are Now in an Immoral Relationship?

Satan would have you believe that there is no hope for you once you have sinned, and because you are unworthy you should just keep committing the sin. This is one of his lies. The woman in John 8:11, who was taken in adultery, was told by our Lord, "Neither do I condemn thee: go, and sin no more." Repent and stop. Repentance begins by seeing your bishop. He holds the keys by which you can go through the repentance process and become clean and worthy again.

There Are Always Consequences

Too often people give away an eternity of happiness for a moment of pleasure. Life presents you with a wooden stick. On one end is written *decisions* and at the other end *consequences*. You cannot pick up one end of the stick without the other. This then is one of the devil's most effective methods for leading you astray. He would have you make decisions without ever considering the consequences.

Conclusion

Perhaps as you read this chapter you thought, *I've heard all of this before.* Let me share with you why the principles in this chapter are so important. Someday you will have to make the most important decision of your life and you will try to determine if you are really in love. Carefully read the following by Elder Hugh W. Pinnock:

> There are not to be sexual experiences before marriage. Temporary pleasure . . . is not worth the incredibly high price of heartache, self-doubt, and guilt, with always the question gnawing at one's spirit, "Is it true love that I am feeling or some sort of hormonal substitute?"[12]

Should you marry while involved in an immoral relationship, you close the door to a temple marriage, and you may marry for lust rather than true love.

One day you can kneel at an altar in a temple and give yourself to the person you have chosen as your eternal companion. There you will both be dressed in white, symbolic of your worthiness to be married forever. Never do anything that would prevent you from entering the temple of God and receiving this wonderful blessing.

Questions for Thought and Discussion

1. Reread Elder Jeffrey R. Holland's statement. Do you believe that the key to romance is following the Lord by being a true disciple? Are there areas in your dating relationships that you might need to change?

2. Sister Susan Tanner gave four suggestions to protect your virtue. How can you apply her counsel into your life right now?

3. If you are in a serious relationship, do you have safeguards you can establish to remain worthy to enter the holy temple? If you have violated the Lord's moral standards, see your bishop immediately.

4. One of the best ways to avoid making decisions in the heat of the moment is to determine beforehand what you will do and will not do. Make a list of what you will do to remain pure and clean. Can you commit to living according to such standards?

Suggested Reading

Boyd K. Packer, "The Fountain of Life", BYU Eighteen Stake Fireside, 29 Mar. 1992.

Jeffrey R. Holland, "Of Souls, Symbols and Sacraments," BYU Speeches, 1989.

David A. Bednar, "We Believe in Being Chaste," *Ensign*, May 2013, 41.

Kenneth W. Matheson, "Fidelity in Marriage: It's More than you Think," *Ensign*, Sept. 2009).

Chapter 9
The Sanctity of Life

Paragraph 5: We declare the means by which mortal life is created to be divinely appointed. We affirm the sanctity of life and of its importance in God's eternal plan.

Introduction

We are reminded in the Proclamation that life is sacred and central to God's plan. It is apparent in our world today that life is not treated as such. The devil is happy when life is ended through tragedies like murder, natural disasters, and abortion. When the great destruction occurred in 3 Nephi, killing many people, a voice was heard from heaven, saying, "Wo, wo, wo unto this people; wo unto the inhabitants of the whole earth, except they shall repent; for the devil laugheth and his angels rejoice, because of the slain of the fair sons and daughters of my people" (3 Nephi 9:2).

In section 59 of the Doctrine and Covenants, the Lord said, "Thou shalt love thy neighbor as thyself. Thou shalt not steal; neither commit adultery, nor kill, nor do anything like unto it" (D&C 59:6).

What might be like unto killing? Elder Neal A. Maxwell has said that as Latter-day Saints we look at social issues differently than those who are of the world: "We sometimes fail to realize how illuminating gospel truths are with regard to so many issues of the day. For instance, given the plan of salvation with our need to experience this mortal school, to acquire a mortal body, and then knowing the very preciousness of human life—we see the awful practice of widespread abortion differently."[1]

Bringing children into this world is a sacred responsibility and is one of the reasons we marry. Are you aware that from 1973—when Roe versus Wade was decided by the US Supreme Court (legalizing abortion)—to 2008, there have been over 54 million abortions performed in the United States? Why so many? Listen to some women who have had abortions and decide which ones you feel are justified:

- "I can't afford to have another child."

- "I already have two children and I don't want to have more."

- "I accidentally got pregnant with my boyfriend and he did not want the baby."

- "I was raped and did not want the child."

- "My doctor told me I could die if I had another baby."

- "I got German measles in my first trimester and didn't want to take the chance of having a deformed or retarded baby."

The English word *abort* literally means to "cut off the existence of someone" or "to cause someone to disappear."[2] We have already discussed in chapter 2 the doctrine that in our premortal life we were spirit children of God. Those who choose to have an abortion for any other reasons than those approved by the Lord are preventing God's spirit children from receiving mortal bodies. They are therefore hindering the Lord's plan of salvation.

What Are Justifiable Reasons for an Abortion?

The Church opposes elective abortion—the voluntary destruction of the fetus in the womb of its mother for non-emergency purposes or nonmedical reasons—for personal or social convenience. Members must not submit to, perform, arrange for, pay for, consent to, or encourage an abortion. The only possible exceptions are when:

- Pregnancy results from forcible rape or incest.

- A competent physician determines that the life or health of the mother is in serious jeopardy.

- A competent physician determines that the fetus has severe defects that will not allow the baby to survive beyond birth.

Church leaders have said, "Even these exceptions do not justify abortion automatically. Abortion is a most serious matter and should be considered only after the persons responsible have consulted with their bishops and received divine confirmation in prayer. . . . Church members who submit to, perform, encourage, pay for, or arrange for an abortion may be subject to Church discipline."[3]

What does the Church recommend for a woman who becomes pregnant out of wedlock? President Gordon B. Hinckley counseled,

> Marriage is the more honorable thing. . . . When marriage is not possible, experience has shown that adoption, difficult though this may be for the young mother, may afford a greater opportunity for the child to live a life of happiness. . . . Abortion is not the answer. This only compounds the problem. It is an evil and repulsive escape that will someday bring regret and remorse.[4]

The most certain way to avoid abortion is to stay morally clean. President Spencer W. Kimball emphasized the sacredness of life when he said,

> My dear young people, there are two very important things I need to say to you about abortion. First, abortion is wrong. Abortion is one of the most revolting and sinful practices in this day, when we are witnessing a frightening increase in permissiveness leading to sexual immorality. How could anyone submit to, encourage, or participate in any way in such an evil act? Second, to those who have so sinned, there may be a way back, not easy, but there may be a way. While forgiveness may be possible, the road back is long and difficult. Do not be deceived—wickedness never will lead to happiness. Some of God's most sacred commandments are violated when a person trifles or interferes with any of the processes of reproduction.[5]

Conclusion

God has declared that life is sacred and we are commanded not to kill or do anything like unto it. Abortion is like unto murder; the way to avoid this serious sin is to keep your God-given powers of procreation sacred.

Questions for Thought and Discussion

1. What can you do to keep your powers of procreation sacred?

2. Do you know anyone that has been involved in an abortion, or have you yourself been involved? Recognize the awful consequences of such choices.

Suggested Reading

Gordon B. Hinckley, "Walking in the Light of the Lord," *Ensign*, Nov. 1998, 99.

Dallin H. Oaks, "The Great Plan of Happiness," *Ensign*, Nov. 1993, 74.

Section II: Deciding Whom to Marry

This section focuses on paragraphs 4 (the first two sentences), 6, 7, 8, and 9 of the Proclamation, from chapters 10 to 20. We will explore important areas that need to be discussed with the person you are considering for marriage. The more compatible you are in these areas, the better the chances will be of your having a successful marriage.

Many people go into a marriage based mainly on physical attraction. This can fade very quickly and soon other qualities—such as personal habits or mental and emotional stability—become of greater importance. The more you can find out about the person you intend to marry before the actual marriage, the better off you will be.

The questions at the end of each chapter will help you find out more about your potential marriage partner.

One caution: because no one is perfect, you need to look for potential in the one you are considering marrying rather than perfection.

Chapter 10
Children Are an Heritage of the Lord

Paragraph 4: The first commandment that God gave to Adam and Eve pertained to their potential for parenthood as husband and wife. We declare that God's commandment for His children to multiply and replenish the earth remains in force.

Introduction

During the April 2011 General Conference, President Monson said, "Where once the standards of the Church and the standards of society were mostly compatible, now there is a wide chasm between us, and it's growing ever wider."[1]

One of the standards he may have been referring to was bearing children, which is one of the most important decisions a Latter-day Saint couple will make when they marry. President Boyd K. Packer made this statement concerning the sealing ceremony in the temple:

> As you understand the sealing ordinance, you will know that the Lord wills that you live together naturally, and that of this relationship children will be born. You are under obligation—it is not just a privilege—of multiplying and replenishing the earth, and in consequence of this the Lord has promised all of the basic essential joys.[2]

Perhaps you have heard people make excuses like finishing school, enjoying time with their spouse before having children, being more financially secure, and so on. These reasons could be made by people not of our faith or by those following the standards of the world relative to children. But we are not to be of the world. We are under covenant to follow the Lord's commandments. Elder Dallin H. Oaks taught,

When married couples postpone childbearing until after they have satisfied their material goals, the mere passage of time assures that they seriously reduce their potential to participate in furthering our Heavenly Father's plan for all His spirit children. Faithful Latter-day Saints cannot afford to look upon children as an interference with what the world calls "self-fulfillment." Our covenants with God and the ultimate purpose of life are tied up in those little ones who reach for our time, our love, and our sacrifices.[3]

Exercising Our Faith

Julie Beck, former general president of the Relief Society, testified,

We believe in the formation of eternal families. That means we believe in getting married. We know that the commandment to multiply and replenish the earth remains in force. That means we believe in having children. We have faith that with the Lord's help we can be successful in rearing and teaching children.[4]

Faith is an assurance that what the Lord teaches us through His prophets is true. This assurance comes from the Holy Spirit. Faith is a gift from Heavenly Father to those seeking to keep their covenants. It gives us hope that the promises of the Lord will be fulfilled. This is true when paying tithing, living the Word of Wisdom, and having children.

How Many Children Should a Couple Have?

Elder Dallin H. Oaks has said, "All they can care for! . . . Exercising faith in God's promises to bless them when they are keeping His commandments, many LDS parents have large families. Others seek but are not blessed with children or with the number of children they desire. In a matter as intimate as this, we should not judge one another."[5]

What about Birth Control?

The following is from the *Encyclopedia of Mormonism* on birth control.

One of the basic teachings of the Church, however, is that spirit children of God come to earth to obtain a physical body, to grow, and to be tested. In that process, adults should marry and provide temporal bodies for those spirit children. For Latter-day Saints, it is a blessing, a joy, and also an obligation to bear children and to raise a family. . . .

The exercise of individual agency is therefore required, and Latter-day Saints believe that personal growth results from weighing the alternatives, studying matters carefully, counseling with appropriate Church leaders, and then seeking inspiration from the Lord before making a decision.

Church members are taught to study the question of family planning, including such important aspects as the physical and mental health of the mother and father and their capacity to provide the basic necessities of life. If, for personal reasons, a couple prayerfully decides that having another child immediately is unwise, birth control may be appropriate. Abstinence, of course, is a form of contraception. Like any other method, however, it has its side effects, some of which may be harmful to the marriage relationship. . . .

Decisions regarding the number and spacing of children are to be made by husband and wife together, in righteousness, and through empathetic communication, and with prayer for the Lord's inspiration.[6]

Conclusion

President David O. McKay taught, "Love realizes its sweetest happiness and most divine consummation in the home where the coming of children is not restricted, where they are made most welcome, and where the duties of parenthood are accepted as a co-partnership with the eternal Creator."[7]

Questions for Thought and Discussion

1. How do you feel about one day having children? Are you and the one you plan to marry in agreement about children?

2. Should you marry someone not of your faith, marital problems often arise with the birth of children. How would you both decide what faith the children would be raised in?

Suggested Reading

Elder Dallin H. Oaks, "Protect the Children," *Ensign*, Nov. 2012.

Dr. Homer Ellsworth, *Ensign*, August 1979, 23.

Chapter 11
How Do You Know It's Love?

Paragraph 6: Husband and wife have a solemn responsibility to love and care for each other and for their children.

Introduction

An important question to ask yourself is, "Am I really in love?" Why ask? Because it is necessary to understand this mysterious feeling we call love. Our happiness in life depends on it.

The word *love* is found five times in the Proclamation: three times in paragraph 6—relating to husband and wife and their children—and two times in paragraph 7, relating to happiness in family life. Love is a central word and concept in the Proclamation. However, in our culture, the word *love* is often misunderstood. Before you decide if you are really in love, you have to understand what love is and what type of love it is, as you will need a love that will withstand the stresses and challenges of marriage.

What Is Love?

Love exists in differing degrees. I like to compare these degrees to the three kingdoms: telestial, terrestrial, and celestial, with celestial love being the highest. Feelings are involved with each degree of love and you need to know what is motivating these feelings. The way to tell what is motivating a particular degree of love is the behavior that it causes.

You have probably heard of puppy love or being infatuated. In a book entitled *Strengthening Our Families*, the authors present the characteristics of an immature love (puppy love) and a mature love.[1] I compare telestial love to an immature love and mature love to a terrestrial love. Look for what is motivating a person to feel either immature or mature love.

	Immature Love	Mature Love
Emotional	Possessiveness, infatuation, jealousy, preoccupation	Lasting passion, a desire for companionship
Belief	Love is external from us and is beyond our control, "love is blind"	Love is something you "decide," sacrifice, trust, commitment, sharing
Behavior	Selfishness, lustful, clingy, concerned with satisfaction of own needs, dependence	Environment of growth and development, allows space for each to grow

A Telestial Love

What can you learn from comparing these two types of love? Did you notice that immature love is based on fulfilling one's own needs, a love of self, or selfishness? It is likely not surprising that the number one reason for divorce, according to our Church Leaders, is selfishness. Note what results from a telestial love:

- Possessiveness

- Jealousy

- Lust

- Dependence

A telestial love motivates a person to take from the one they feel they love. Often people in such a love relationship will say, "I can't live without her" or, "If he leaves me, I will never be happy." The main reason for such strong feelings is usually because the person is in a sexual relationship. However, people can get over the hurt that comes from a "telestial breakup." It usually takes sincere and humble repentance. People with a telestial love must also realize that after they leave the sexual relationship and try to repent, the devil will tempt them to go back into the relationship, thus negating their

65

repentance. Of course, the best method for happiness and safety with regards to love is to never be in a sexual relationship before marriage.

A Terrestrial Love

A mature love is more stable and concerned with the growth and happiness of others. It is a great challenge to develop a mature love because it requires sustained effort and sacrifice.

Mature love can be compared to a terrestrial love because it will usually last throughout a lifetime. It can be characterized by a deep, abiding friendship between husband and wife and is often based on the teachings of Jesus Christ as found in the Bible. Note the words that describe a mature love:

- A desire for companionship

- An environment of growth and development

- Allows space for each to grow

A Celestial Love

Yet it seems to me that Jesus Christ and the prophets talk about a degree of love above mature. In the scriptures it is known as "the pure love of Christ," or charity. *The LDS Bible Dictionary* defines charity as "the highest, noblest, strongest kind of love, not merely affection; the pure love of Christ."[2] This type of love is eternal; it endures trials, hardships, and all the challenges married couples face. It is based on the teachings of Christ. This type of love has at least these three characteristics:

1. It is a gift of the Spirit to those who love God and keep His commandments (see Moroni 7:45).

2. It will not end at death and is the quality of love possessed by those who inherit the celestial kingdom. (See Moroni 8:25–26).

3. This love, sometimes called charity in the scriptures, has thirteen qualities. Mormon described these qualities to help us understand what the fruits of this love are.

Carefully review and think on the following table:

Quality	Possible Meaning
Suffers long	Patient
Is kind	Sensitive
Does not envy	Supportive
Is not puffed up	Humble
Does not seek its own	Unselfish
Is not easily provoked	Controls anger
Does not think evil	Trusting of others
Does not rejoice in iniquity	Righteous
Rejoices in the truth	Honest
Bears all things	Submissive to direction
Believes all things	Faithful
Hopes all things	Optimistic
Endures all things	Submits to trials

To acquire each of the above qualities, we need the Holy Ghost. This precious gift is bestowed on those who are striving to be disciples of Jesus Christ. As we try to keep the commandments, the Holy Ghost helps us to become Christ-like.

Statements by Church Leaders about Charity

Here are some statements by modern prophets and apostles that describe this quality of love.

President Gordon B. Hinckley: "True love is not so much a matter of romance as it is a matter of anxious concern for the well-being of one's companion."[3]

Elder Richard G. Scott: "Love, as defined by the Lord, elevates, protects, respects, and enriches another. It motivates one to make sacrifices for another."[4]

President Thomas S. Monson: "Love is the balm that brings healing to the soul. But love doesn't grow like weeds or fall like rain. Love has its price. 'God so loved the world, that He gave His Only Begotten Son, that whosoever believeth in Him should not perish, but have everlasting life' (John 3:16). That Son, even the Lord Jesus

Christ, gave His life that we might have eternal life, so great was His love for His Father and for us."[5]

Elder Marvin J. Ashton: "True love is a process. True love requires personal action. Love must be continuing to be real. Love takes time. Too often expediency, infatuation, stimulation, persuasion, or lust are mistaken for love. How hollow, how empty if our love is no deeper than the arousal of momentary feelings or expressions in words of what is more lasting than the time it takes to speak them."[6]

President Spencer W. Kimball: "If one really loves another, one would rather die for that person than to injure him [or her]. At the hour of sin, pure love is pushed out of one door while lust sneaks in the other. Affection has then been replaced with desire of the flesh and uncontrolled passion. Accepted has been the doctrine which the devil is so eager to establish, that illicit sexual relations are justified."[7]

Jesus Exemplified Charity

During His earthly ministry, Christ described love as selflessness.

- "Love another; as I have loved you" (John 13:34).

- "God so loved the world, that He gave His Only Begotten Son" (John 3:16).

- "Ye are my disciples, if ye have love one to another" (John 13:35).

- "Greater love hath no man than this, that a man lay down his life for his friends" (John 15:13).

Love, as Jesus taught, is something we give rather than get. It is much more than a feeling; it includes *action*. When you take action, you will have found one of the greatest keys to a happy life and marriage. Our Heavenly Father so loved each of us that He "gave" His Only Begotten Son as a sacrifice for each of us. Jesus's entire ministry was focused on giving.

Which type of love do you want when you marry? If someone says he or she loves you, do his or her actions prove it?

Comparison of the Three Degrees of Love

Let's look at what motivates each degree of love as well as the actions and behaviors it begets.

Type	Motivation / Feeling	Actions / Behaviors
Telestial	I want to have my needs satisfied	Sexual relations, jealousy of relationships the partner has, no personal space, arguing
Terrestrial	I want for us to become best friends	Seek to work problems out, allow for personal space to grow, concern for the other's needs and wants
Celestial	I want to follow the Lord and be worthy of being with you forever	Center of the relationship is the Lord, repent when they hurt each other

Now, don't become discouraged because you might not possess all of the qualities of the pure love of Christ. His pure love is developed and acquired over time by keeping the Lord's commandments, serving others, remaining faithful to the Lord during trials and challenges, and consistently praying for the Lord's Spirit in your life. People who marry are not usually soulmates. That is just a myth. Married people become soulmates over time through love and devotion to each other and to the Lord.

Elder Spencer W. Kimball taught about the importance of preparing for marriage. "The successful marriage depends in large measure upon the preparation made in approaching it. . . . One cannot pick the ripe, rich, luscious fruit from a tree that was never planted, nurtured, nor pruned."[8]

One of the best ways you can prepare for marriage, should you desire a celestial marriage, is taking the time to really get to know the person you feel you are in love with and evaluate if Jesus Christ is the center of your relationship.

Conclusion

Knowing the different levels of love, how can you tell if the love you are developing has the capacity to grow into a celestial love that will last forever? I believe President David O. McKay described it well:

> You may ask, "How do I know when I am in love?" This is a very important question. A fellow student and I considered that query

one night as we walked together. As boys of that age frequently do, we were talking about girls. Neither he nor I knew whether or not we were in love. Of course I had not then met my present sweetheart. In answer to my question, "How may we know when we are in love?" he replied: "My mother once said that if you meet a girl in whose presence you feel a desire to achieve, who inspires you to do your best, and to make the most of yourself, such a young woman is worthy of your love and is awakening love in your heart.[9]

I can tell you—without any reservations—that this guideline by President McKay is true.

Questions for Thought and Discussion

1. How can you better overcome selfishness and look for opportunities to serve and help others?

2. Learn to be sensitive to the needs of other people. What could you do today to notice people around you and how you might lessen their burdens?

3. How do you treat the people you date? Are you demanding, selfish, jealous? Is lust the basis of your relationship?

4. If you are in a serious relationship, are you developing patterns of kindness, honesty, and service to each other?

5. Does the person you feel you might marry bring out the best in you? Does he or she help you draw closer to the Lord? If not, you might reconsider your feelings.

Suggested Reading

Elder Bruce C. Hafen, "Beauty for Ashes: The Atonement of Jesus Christ," *Ensign*, March 1974, 3; "The Gospel and Romantic Love," *Ensign*, Oct. 1982.

Marlin K. Jensen, "A Union of Love and Understanding," *Ensign*, October 1994, 46.

Thomas S. Monson, "Love—the Essence of the Gospel," *Ensign*, May 2014, 91.

Chapter 12
The Sacred Duty of Parenthood

Paragraph 6: "Children are an heritage of the Lord" (Psalm 127:3). Parents have a sacred duty to rear their children in love and righteousness, to provide for their physical and spiritual needs, and to teach them to love and serve one another, observe the commandments of God, and be law-abiding citizens wherever they live. Husbands and wives—mothers and fathers—will be held accountable before God for the discharge of these obligations.

Introduction

An important subject to discuss with someone you feel you are in love with is how you will parent children. Heavenly Father and Jesus Christ love little children, "for of such is the kingdom of heaven" (Matthew 19:14). To one who would hurt or injure children, He said, "It were better for him that a millstone were hanged about his neck, and that he were drowned in the depth of the sea" (Matthew 18:6). One of God's great concerns is how His spirit children come into this mortal life and how they are cared for.

A Serious Responsibility

As you are aware, one of your purposes for being here on earth is to bring God's spirit children into mortality. This is a serious responsibility. The Proclamation calls it "a sacred duty." The choices you are making right now will one day affect the kind of parent you will be. When Elijah appeared to the Prophet Joseph Smith, he said the keys he held would turn the hearts of children to their fathers, and the hearts

71

of fathers to their children. Though you are probably not yet a father or a mother, you can have your heart turn to your future children now by preparing in the Lord's way for parenthood. These precious souls are waiting to come to you at the right time and in the right way.

President Thomas S. Monson emphasized the importance of parenthood: "As parents, we should remember that our lives may be the book from the family library which the children most treasure. Are our examples worthy of emulation? Do we live in such a way that a son or a daughter may say, "I want to follow my dad," or "I want to be like my mother"? Unlike the book on the library shelf, the covers of which shield the contents, our lives cannot be closed. Parents, we truly are an open book in the library of learning of our homes."[1]

Preparing for Parenthood

The Proclamation provides guidance on how you may prepare for parenthood. It gives five qualities of effective parenting and also a warning to consider as you prepare for marriage and family.

Rear your children in love and righteousness.

You can prepare to do this by learning to love and serve little children. Also, the relationships you have with your family, friends, and associates provide you with opportunities to overcome the human tendency of selfishness. Inviting children into your future home will require you to think more of them than you do of yourself. Such qualities as forgiveness, selflessness, and patience are essential to rearing children in a home of love. As you seek now to keep the covenants you have made, you are preparing to lead your children in righteousness. Being a parent is not only a great challenge but a divine calling. It is an effort requiring consecration.

President James E. Faust said, "The teaching, rearing, and training of children requires more intelligence, intuitive understanding, humility, strength, wisdom, spirituality, perseverance, and hard work than any other challenge we might have in life."[2]

One of the qualities you will want to look for in a future companion is how he or she feels about and relates to children of all ages.

Provide for their physical and spiritual needs.

Explicitly stated in the Proclamation, when you are a parent it will not be enough to just provide for the physical needs of children.

Their spiritual needs are as important as their physical ones. When children become part of your home, they will be totally dependent on you and they will have both physical and spiritual needs.

Our children's spiritual needs are nourished through the gospel. Activities such as family home evening, family prayer, scripture study, and Church attendance are just some of the ways this can be accomplished. What you are learning in your secular education and through Church meetings will help prepare you for this responsibility.

Teach them to love and serve one another.

It is not unusual for brothers and sisters to fight and bicker with each other. The solution to this challenge is right in the Proclamation. If siblings would seek to love and serve each other, such fighting and arguing would probably be eliminated, or at least lessened. Jesus gave a marvelous promise to those who would seek to be peacemakers. He said, "Blessed are the peacemakers: for they shall be called the children of God" (Matthew 5:9). Did you notice that Jesus made this promise to those who would seek to *make* peace? The way you and your spouse treat each other will do more than what you say in words. Kindness, sensitivity, and frequent expressions of love will be even more important.

Teach them to observe the commandments of God.

Some young people see the commandments as being restrictive. Actually, the commandments are the means to freedom. Jesus said, "Ye shall know the truth, and the truth shall make you free" (John 8:32). When you keep the commandments you are free to receive the Holy Ghost to guide you, free from harmful addictions, free to partake worthily of the sacrament, free to enter the holy temple, and free to have God's blessings upon you and your eternal companion. The attitude you have right now toward the commandments will influence how you teach them to your children.

Teach them to be law-abiding citizens wherever they live.

Have you noticed that three of the five parental responsibilities have to do with teaching? The best way to teach is by example. Your example will have a more powerful impact on your children than what you say. Do you have respect for the laws of the land in which you live and those who administer the laws? Your children will watch your example and will, in many instances, follow it.

A Warning to Parents

In 1980, the First Presidency and the Quorum of the Twelve issued a proclamation to the Church, "We affirm the sanctity of the family as a divine creation and declare that God our Eternal Father will hold parents accountable to rear their children in light and truth."[3]

In 1995, fifteen prophets, seers, and revelators issued another warning: "Husbands and wives—mothers and fathers—will be held accountable before God for the discharge of these obligations." As a parent, you will be held accountable for how you teach and raise your children. You will *not* be held accountable for how your children turn out. They have their agency. In the Doctrine and Covenants the Lord has said, "And again, inasmuch as parents have children in Zion, or in any of her stakes, which are organized, that teach them not to understand the doctrine of repentance, faith in Christ the Son of the living God, and of baptism and the gift of the Holy Ghost by the laying on of hands, when eight years old, the sin be upon the head of the parents" (D&C 68:25).

Conclusion

Right now you are preparing to one day become a parent. The gospel can assist you in this great responsibility. Relief Society and priesthood meetings have been a great help to my wife and me as we have tried to raise our children in the ways of the Lord.

President Gordon B. Hinckley said, "A nation will rise no higher than the strength of its homes. If you want to reform a nation, you begin with families, with parents who teach their children principles and values that are positive and affirmative and will lead them to worthwhile endeavors."[4]

Questions for Thought and Discussion

1. Discuss together what being a good parent means and the five areas of parenting described in the Proclamation. How might you apply them in your future parenting?

Suggested Reading

L. Tom Perry, "Obedience Brings Blessings," *Ensign*, May 2013.

Chapter 13
Commitments and Covenants

Paragraph 7: The family is ordained of God. Marriage between man and woman is essential to His eternal plan. Children are entitled to birth within the bonds of matrimony, and to be reared by a father and a mother who honor marital vows with complete fidelity.

Introduction

Have you ever had a friend say, "I'll meet you at 7 p.m." Then you wait until 9 p.m. and he or she still hasn't come? We call people who frequently do not keep their commitments flaky, unreliable, and irresponsible. An important characteristic of a marriage partner is that he or she keeps commitments.

President Spencer W. Kimball said, "A beginning [to influencing our children for good] is a secure marriage, where there is a commitment to make the personal adjustments to live together forever."[1]

What Does It Mean to Be Committed?

An important quality of a successful marriage is the commitment the couple brings to the marriage. The word commitment refers to an obligation that restricts freedom of action.[2] When we make a commitment, we are not free to do something else. Two synonyms are loyalty and faithfulness. Some couples marry and divorce because they did not enter marriage with a strong commitment to be loyal and faithful to each other no matter the challenges they might face. The scriptures teach the importance of enduring to the end, and because marriage is hard work, you will need to *endure* many challenges that will require commitment, sacrifice, and loyalty to your partner.

Differences between Covenants and Commitments

In the Church, the difference between a covenant and a commitment is that covenants are between us and the Lord while commitments are made between people. In the ordinances of the gospel, the Lord determines the covenants we make and the blessings associated with keeping those covenants. We can always count on the Lord keeping His part of the covenant. The challenge is for us to keep our part. The sacramental ordinance is an excellent example of a covenant, as we promise to do certain things and the Lord promises us the companionship of the Holy Ghost if we keep our covenants.

When you marry in the temple, you will also make covenants with the Lord. Therefore, one way to determine whom to marry is to ask yourself this question: "How well does he or she keep gospel covenants?" Does he or she keep baptismal covenants by keeping the commandments and serving others? If he or she is flaky or unreliable, you had better clear that up before marriage or you could face many challenges after. One of the purposes of dating is to give you insight into the integrity and habits of those you date.

What Is Your Commitment to Your Children?

The Proclamation states that when you marry and bring children into this world, they are "entitled" to being born into a family where a man and a woman are married and being raised by a father and mother who are true and faithful (committed) to the covenant of marriage.

One of the reasons people live together without marrying is they are fearful of making a commitment to marriage and family. Without a commitment, the couple may feel free to do their own thing. Couples who enter marriage with a firm commitment to keep their covenants with God and with each other will have a much better chance of having a successful marriage.

Honoring Marriage Covenants with Fidelity

There is a growing problem affecting marriages in the Church. President Gordon B. Hinckley indicated,

For a full decade now I have participated in the task of sitting in judgment on the worthiness of those who plead to come back into the Church after having been excommunicated. In every case there had been a serious violation of Church standards of conduct. In most cases there had been adultery.[3]

Adultery is one of the primary reasons for the increased destruction of marriages and families in today's society. You live in an "anti-chastity culture," where movies, TV, and other forms of entertainment glorify adultery as an exciting adventure and, in some cases, a normal thing. Many children today live in a home where adultery was the reason for their parents separating.

The term *chastity* is used when people who are not married reserve sexual relations for when they are. *Fidelity* is used for married couples who reserve sexual relations only for each other. What then can you do to help ensure that there is total fidelity in your marriage?

The first thing is to remain totally chaste before you marry. It may not come as a surprise that people who engage in sexual relations with any number of people before marriage are more likely to commit adultery after. This is particularly true in regards to men. The root problem is lust, which is the opposite of "the beautiful and holy word of love."[4]

Elder Hugh W. Pinnock said, "Obedience . . . is the sure cornerstone of happiness. A boyfriend or girlfriend who does not have a wholesome respect for regulations during the dating process will often continue to break the rules after the word *yes* at the altar is spoken. Seek out those who are willing to live the rules."[5]

When children are born into a family, they are totally innocent and pure, having come to this earth with light and truth. How then does the adversary take away that light and truth they come here with? Doctrine and Covenants 93:39: "And that wicked one cometh and taketh away light and truth, through disobedience, from the children of men, and because of *the traditions of their fathers*." (Italics added.) "Traditions of their fathers" are the customs, habits, and beliefs that parents pass on to their children. You must decide now what traditions you will pass on to your children. If you are committed to having a morally clean life, free of addictions and bad habits, you will have a better chance of a healthy, lasting marriage and your children will not have to face the challenges that come with divorce. You owe it to your future children to keep the covenants you make with the Lord.

Conclusion

At one time my wife and I were service missionaries in our stake. One of our assignments was the addiction recovery program, with an emphasis on those addicted to pornography. One evening while I met with a group of men, one mentioned he was engaged. After the group meeting, he and I were chatting and I asked, "When are you getting married?" He responded, "I am not sure. My fiancée will not marry me until I have shown I am really committed to staying free of pornography." She must have been a smart young woman. She wanted to marry a man who would keep his commitments.

Questions for Thought and Discussion

1. How have you kept the covenants you made at baptism? Should you choose to marry someone who has not been faithful to his or her covenants, that could be a red flag for future problems.

2. Look over this chapter with the one you intend to marry. What does he or she think it means to be faithful? Discuss what you will do to remain faithful to each other.

3. Read the following by Elder David B. Haight with the one you are considering as a marriage partner: "A strong, shared conviction that there is something eternally precious about a marriage relationship builds faith to resist evil."[6] How do both you and the one you intend to marry feel about this "shared conviction"? How can such a conviction help you resist evil?

4. If there have been problems of immorality, have they been repented of before marriage? Read *The Miracle of Forgiveness* by President Spencer W. Kimball.

Suggested Reading

Gordon B. Hinckley, "Walking in the Light of the Lord," *Ensign,* Nov. 1998, 99.

Kenneth W. Matheson, "Fidelity is More than You Think," *Ensign*, Sept. 2009.

Chapter 14
Inviting Christ into Your Marriage

Paragraph 7: Happiness in family life is most likely to be achieved when founded upon the teachings of the Lord Jesus Christ.

Introduction

Some years ago, I had a dream that caused me great concern. I must admit that I have not had many dreams that I thought were inspired, and I am not sure this one was. I dreamed I was in a room waiting for someone to come in and join me. A door opened and an individual came in and said, "Robert, how are you?" Somewhat embarrassed, I replied, "You seem to know me, but who are you?" The person replied, "I am your Savior, Jesus Christ." As I remember, I woke up with a start, wondering if I was being given a message. There are two questions each of us needs to ask ourselves: How well do I know my Savior Jesus Christ, and why is it important to know Him?"

An Analogy about Marriage and Family

Elder Robert D. Hales of the Quorum of the Twelve Apostles, in a talk given at a fireside, compared marriage to climbing a mountain. "Marriage is like climbing a mountain. You tie yourself to a companion, and you start up the mountain of life. As a child comes along, you tie him to mom and dad and continue your journey. . . . But there are many elements—the wind and the rain and the snow and the ice—all the elements of the world will tear at you to pull you off that eternal mountain. How do you reach the summit?"[1]

Christ taught that when we build our marriage and family on His teachings, the rains and winds that inevitable come will not make our marriages and families fall. (See Matthew 7: 24–29 and Helaman 5:12.)

How Can Christ Bless Your Marriage and Family?

When my wife and I first married, we determined that to have a happy, healthy, and successful marriage we would need to follow the teachings of Jesus Christ given in the scriptures and from our Church leaders. (See D&C 1:38.) This meant having family home evening and family prayer, going to Church, doing scripture study together, and being obedient to the commandments.

Jesus said, "Therefore, whoso heareth these sayings of mine and *doeth* them, I will liken him unto a wise man who built his house upon a rock." Those who did not follow His teachings, He compared to "a foolish man who built his house upon sand" (3 Nephi 14:24, 26; italics added).

Elder Howard W. Hunter, in a general conference, used the New Testament story of Jairus to teach an important principle. Jairus's daughter lay sick to the point of death and he appealed to Jesus to come and heal her. Jesus went and took her by the hand, lifted her up, and she lived. (See Mark 5: 22–24.) Elder Hunter then said, "Whatever Jesus lays His hands upon, lives. If He lays His hands upon a marriage, it lives. If He is allowed to lay His hands on the family, it lives."[2]

I have a personal testimony that what Elder Hunter taught is true. When I make Jesus Christ the center of my life and priorities, I am a better person, a better husband, and a better father and grandfather. Why? Because as I follow His teachings, I seek to repent of wrongdoings and try to be more patient, loving, and caring; I strive to become more like Him.

Elder Hugh W. Pinnock said, "The most fulfilling of all marriages that I have observed seem to be those in which the husband and wife together commit their love to the Savior's keeping and to each other."[3]

Faith in Jesus Christ

To invite Jesus into your life and marriage requires trust in Him. Faith is trust, and when we trust Jesus we will do what He asks us to do. Why? Because we know that His only desire is that we be happy with our lives and marriages. In 3 Nephi 12–14 are found the beatitudes Jesus taught the Nephite people. The word *beatitude* means "how happy are." The beatitudes then become Jesus's formula for happiness, so you may wish to study these chapters.

Conclusion

Our Savior said, "Come unto me, all ye that labour and are heavy laden and I will give you rest. Take my yoke upon you [become His disciple], . . . for my yoke is easy, and my burden is light" (Matthew 11:28–30).

Questions for Thought and Discussion

1. Where does Jesus fit into your personal priorities?

2. How does focusing on Jesus help with marriage? Discuss this with an active, committed married couple.

3. Consider a personal scripture study program to read 3 Nephi. What does it teach you about Jesus Christ?

4. How you will keep Christ the center of your marriage? Talk it over with the one you are considering as a marriage partner.

Chapter 15
Nine Foundation Stones for Marriage

Paragraph 7: Successful marriages and families are established and maintained on principles of faith, prayer, repentance, forgiveness, respect, love, compassion, work, and wholesome recreational activities.

Introduction

When the Saints arrived in the Salt Lake Valley in 1849, one of the first things President Brigham Young did was to dedicate a place for a temple. Once the tedious and time-consuming work of laying the foundation was done, Brigham Young was informed that there was a problem. The workmen had used a soft stone for the foundation. The work was stopped and the soft stone removed, replaced with giant blocks of granite. President Young said, "We are building a temple to stand through the millennium."[1] Likewise, you will want to build your marriage on a solid foundation that will last forever.

Nine Foundation Stones

The Proclamation gives you nine solid granite stones upon which to build your marriage and to use to evaluate a relationship *before* marriage. Each of these stones is important so that your marriage can withstand the stresses and challenges that will come. You can choose to build your marriage and family on soft stone or on granite. A foundation of soft stone will not endure for eternity and probably not even "until death do you part." An eternal marriage must be built on solid granite.

Granite Stone #1: Faith

Elder Dallin H. Oaks said, "Faith must include trust . . ."[2] Marriages based on trust in the Lord place Him at the very center of marriage and family. These couples frequently ask, "What would the Savior have us do?" The commandments of the Lord thus become central to this family. Faith in the Lord and in one another give a couple something to hold onto when challenges inevitably come.

Elder David B. Haight, a former apostle, added, "Marriage is sustained by faith and knowledge of its divine establishment, and is sustained daily by the energy of love."[3]

Faith in the Lord also includes trust in those who represent Him. The Lord has said that "whether by mine own voice or by the voice of my servants, it is the same" (D&C 1:38). One of the great evidences of God's love for us is that He calls people to serve and assist. From parents to prophets and apostles to our stake president, bishop, home and visiting teachers, we have people with specific stewardship from God to support and bless us. If we seek their counsel, they can be a great blessing. Do you and your intended marital partner have faith in the Lord Jesus Christ and in His servants?

Granite Stone #2: Prayer

Prayer is our pathway to God and He is ready to guide us. Elder David A. Bednar has suggested three principles to help our prayers become more meaningful:

- Prayer becomes more meaningful as we counsel with the Lord in all our doings (see Alma 37:37).

- Prayer is more meaningful when we express heartfelt gratitude.

- Prayer becomes more meaningful as we pray for others with real intent and a sincere heart.[4]

Not only is daily individual prayer vital but when couples pray together it solidifies their marriage and helps them stay close to each other and to Heavenly Father. Do you trust in your Heavenly Father through regular, daily personal prayer?

President Ezra Taft Benson said, "Family prayer is a consistent practice [in successful families]. Prayer is the means to acknowledge appreciation for blessings and to humbly recognize dependence on Almighty God for strength, sustenance, and support."[5]

Praying for each other is also important. My wife once shared an experience she had with prayer. She told me that I had done something that hurt her deeply. She got on her knees and asked the Lord to zap me so I would feel her hurt. Instead, the inspiration came to bake me a chocolate cake with white frosting (my favorite dessert). She baked the cake and we were able to talk it through and resolve her feelings. Pray for and about each other.

Elder Richard G. Scott said, "A happy marriage results from making correct choices prayerfully together. It can transform a house into a place of heaven on earth."[6]

Granite Stone #3: Repentance

This stone builds on the first two. When we have faith, or trust, in Heavenly Father and pray to Him in the name of His Son, we will desire to change those things within us that are contrary to His will and commandments. Repentance is really the changing of attitudes and habits with the help of our Savior. I think of repentance as making personal course corrections in our lives. Repentance is not trying to change your partner! People who marry thinking they can change their partner are usually very disappointed. Know that the character of the person you marry may not change, even after all of your efforts. This is where the gospel helps a marriage. If you marry someone who is committed to the Lord, the chances are better that he or she will repent of things that need to be changed. *It is all about changing ourselves.* Repentance, therefore, is a key to a happy, successful marriage. Have you found the peace that comes from sincerely repenting of things that need to be changed?

One of the stumbling blocks to repentance is pride. President Ezra Taft Benson advised, "Think of the repentance that could take place with lives changed, marriages preserved, and homes strengthened, if pride did not keep us from confessing our sins and forsaking them."[7]

Granite Stone #4: Forgiveness

Surely this is one of the most fundamental principles of any relationship. All of us make mistakes and do things for which we are sorry. What a relief it is when someone we love and care for forgives us. Yet for some it is difficult to forgive others, and they hold grudges and remember for years the negative things people have done. It is impossible to create a celestial marriage without forgiveness. What is the gospel solution? Simply let go of grudges and seek to forgive and forget. Simple, right? But certainly sometimes this is not easy and may take time. President Hinckley said, "Forgiveness is a mark of divinity."[8] The inability to forgive is one of the major stumbling blocks to a happy marriage and family, but through the Atonement of Jesus Christ we can receive help in forgiving all who have offended us. Indeed we must, for the Lord has said, "I, the Lord, will forgive whom I will forgive, but of you it is *required* to forgive all men" (D&C 64:10; italics added).

President Joseph F. Smith wrote, "Sometimes the husband sees a failing in his wife, and he upbraids [scolds] her with it. Sometimes the wife feels that her husband has not done just the right thing, and she upbraids him. What good does it do? Is not forgiveness better? . . . Is it not better to drop them and say nothing about them—bury them and speak only of the good that you know and feel, and thus bury each other's faults and not magnify them; isn't that better?"[9]

Granite Stone #5: Respect

Respect is one of the basics of any relationship, for without respect there is neither trust nor confidence. But what is "respect" exactly? The dictionary defines respect as "to regard highly," or "to place in high esteem because of a person's character."[10] Doctrine and Covenants 107:4 uses the word *reverence* as a synonym for respect with regards to our relationship with God.

The following example illustrates two aspects of respect: A husband, in a moment of weakness, said something unkind to his wife. She responded, "Why would you say that to me? I'm a nice person!" One way to show respect is in how we treat others. In this case, the husband was disrespectful to his wife. On the other hand, the wife had "self-respect," which was a high regard for herself as being nice. When you truly love and respect someone, you would never intentionally try to hurt them. When we understand that every person we associate with has a divine nature and the potential to become as God, we cannot help but have respect for them.

Self-respect is developed and nourished by doing the things we know to be right. When we choose to disobey our conscience and the covenants we have made, self-respect goes down. It is closely associated with virtue and obedience. When self-respect is low, the devil has a greater chance of getting us to follow him. Self-respect is evidenced in the way we dress, talk, and behave toward others. The Proclamation helps us understand how to respect and value ourselves. We have already seen that we have a divine nature and destiny. Each granite stone before this one—faith, prayer, repentance and forgiveness—leads to self-respect.

A healthy respect for ourselves motivates us to treat other people with a similar respect and dignity. Why? Because we know that all people are children of God with great potential. Respect for Heavenly Father is shown by the way we talk about Him, the way we keep His commandments, and our reverence toward Him.

Granite Stone #6: Love

The Prophet Joseph Smith said, "Nothing is so much calculated to lead people to forsake sin as to take them by the hand and to watch over them with tenderness. When persons manifest the least kindness and love to me, O what power it has over my mind, while the opposite course has a tendency to harrow up all the harsh feelings and depress the human mind."[11]

Love, when referring to relationships, is a verb and therefore must be acted upon to exist. Love, like a flower, is a living thing. If nourished, it can grow; if not nourished, it can die. Four ways to express love are showing kindness, communicating appreciation, making time to talk, and serving each other. Let's look at each of these.

First, kindness is one of the most essential characteristics of a loving person. People are normally forgiving of many things about someone if that person is kind. The opposite of kindness is meanness, usually expressed by talking down to another person or raising of his or her voice. I have read that some marriage counselors have said meanness is one of the most deadly poisons to love. Women often have an ability to remember things better than men, and an explosive, mean argument can be carried with them for years. Something you can do when you marry is make a "commitment to each other that you will never intentionally hurt each other's feelings."[12]

President Ezra Taft Benson continues, "Successful families have love and respect for each family member. Family members know they are loved and appreciated. Children feel they are loved by their parents. Thus, they are secure and self-assured."[13]

Second, appreciation is a fruit of love, essential to a happy marriage. Selfish, inward-looking people rarely show appreciation because they think the world revolves around their wants and needs. Appreciation can be shown in a number of ways, many simple: saying "thank you" or "I love you" or just telling someone they are important to you. Appreciation can also be communicated through actions such as a gift, a note of appreciation, a letter, or an email of gratitude.

Third, a couple must *make* time to talk with each other. Many couples drift apart simply because after marriage they stop talking. Your marriage needs to be your first priority, more important than family, friends, television, working out, or anything else. Because of the world's pressure to push couples apart, this must be a major commitment you make to each other. One solution my wife and I have found very helpful is the "Friday night date." During our date, we talk about our feelings, desires, and challenges. This date has helped us stay in love for over fifty years.

An issue arises if either partner is not willing to talk or to take the time to listen. In my own family it was a sort of custom to not talk about our feelings. Learning to talk is one thing in my marriage I have had to learn to do.

Fourth, keep serving each other. Someone once said that it is not the big things that keep love alive; it's the little things. Doing little things as husband and wife such as sharing household duties or going the extra mile to relieve each other's burdens. There are so many ways in marriage to serve each other. President Ezra Taft Benson said, "Strong families cultivate an attribute of effective communication. They talk out their problems, make plans together, and cooperate toward common objectives. Family home evening and family councils are practiced and used as effective tools toward this end."[14]

Granite Stone #7: Compassion

The word *compassion* means "with feeling." It refers to our ability to feel what others are feeling. Possibly the greatest attribute of God is His compassion for us, His children. Alma indicated that Jesus Christ suffered in the flesh for us that He might know "how to succor His people according to their infirmities" (Alma 7:12). Our Lord's compassion moves Him to run to us when we are in distress. Compassion is an element of charity, the pure love of Christ, and is a gift of the Spirit.

Often we think we are too busy or distracted to try to feel what others are feeling. Men are not usually as good as women at being compassionate (at least this is what some women have told me); they would rather fix a problem than take the time to understand and feel what another feels. Ironically, one of a wife's greatest needs is to have her husband show compassion by feeling what she is feeling. Compassion is essential in a happy marriage and family. When a spouse or children know that what they are feeling has been communicated and received, trust and love grow. One word can help us to have greater compassion and that is *attention*. To really have compassion, we must give the one we love our full attention, free from television or other things that interrupt us. One woman told me that she thought her husband felt he was married to the television for time and eternity! That relationship probably has many challenges.

Granite Stone #8: Work

The Lord said to Adam, when he was cast out of the Garden of Eden, "In the sweat of thy face shalt thou eat bread" (Genesis 3:19). Work has been the hallmark of God's righteous children since the beginning of time. In 1936, when the U.S. administration was introducing public welfare, President Heber J. Grant announced the Church Welfare Program and said, "Work is to be re-enthroned as the ruling principle of the lives of Church membership."[15]

Bishop Keith McMullin added, "Work is physical, mental, or spiritual effort. . . . Work is the source of happiness, self esteem, and prosperity."[16]

Heavenly Father has told us that He has a work to perform. "This is my *work* and my glory—to bring to pass the immortality and eternal life of man" (Moses 1:39; italics added). In the Church we talk about missionary *work*, temple *work*, and family history *work*. So naturally, marriage is work. Elder Dean L. Larsen, former member of the Quorum of the Seventy, cautioned,

> Marriage is not an easy venture. It is largely a one-time-through, do-it-yourself project for the husband and wife. I repeatedly encounter the illusion today, especially among younger people, that perfect marriages happen simply if the right two people come together. This is untrue. Marriages don't succeed automatically. Those who build happy, secure, successful marriages pay the price to do so. They work at it constantly.[17]

Marriage counselor and retired BYU professor Douglas Brinley has written about the word *work* in the Proclamation:

This must include employment and earning income, along with a work ethic. Bills are ever-present and expenses must be met. Children need chores and meaningful assignments in the family. The Lord rebuked early Church leaders because their children lacked a work ethic: "Now, I, the Lord, am not well pleased with the inhabitants of Zion, for there are idlers among them; and their children are also growing up in wickedness" (D&C 68:31).[18]

Elder Neal A. Maxwell has counseled, "Work is always a spiritual necessity even if, for some, work is not an economic necessity."[19]

Granite Stone #9: Wholesome Recreational Activities

Why would the Proclamation include wholesome recreational activities? Is there a time in marriage when we need to take off our work clothes and have an enjoyable time together?

Read carefully. The Proclamation does not say "fun recreational activities" but "wholesome" ones. Things like movies, music, and dance clubs can be fun but not always the most wholesome activity to be doing. How then do you determine what is wholesome? In the Book of Mormon, Moroni quotes from a letter his father, Mormon, wrote to him. In the letter, Mormon gives you a formula to judge what is wholesome from what is not. Look for the three criteria Mormon gives:

> But behold, that which is of God inviteth and enticeth to do good continually; wherefore, every thing which inviteth and enticeth to do good, and to love God, and to serve him, is inspired of God. . . . But whatsoever thing persuadeth men to do evil, and believe not in Christ, and deny him, and serve not God, then ye may know with a perfect knowledge it is of the devil (Moroni 7:13, 17).

Did you find the three criteria for judging what is wholesome?

1. Does this activity influence me to keep the commandments and follow the counsel of the Lord and His servants?

2. Do I feel closer to God because of this?

3. Do I feel like praying, going to Church, and serving the Lord because of this activity?

Some people lose the power to judge what is wholesome because they have been so involved in unwholesome activity that they can no longer tell right from wrong. It has been said you can't feel the wind blow when you're lying down. Likewise, you can't feel the effects of sin if you are going along with it. Those who say, "That was not so bad," or, "I hear worse at school" could be going along with the winds of sin. Elder H. Burke Peterson, former member of the Seventy, said,

> Stay away from any movie, video, publication, or music—*regardless of its rating*—where illicit behavior and expressions are a part of the action. Have the courage to turn it off in your living room. Throw the tapes and the publications in the garbage can, for that is where we keep garbage. . . . Again I say, leave it alone. Turn it off, walk away from it, burn it, erase it, destroy it. I know it is hard counsel we give when we say movies that are R-rated, and many with PG-13 ratings, are produced by satanic influences. Our standards should not be dictated by the rating system.[20]

Wholesome recreational activities provide wonderful memories for family members. Elder Marion D. Hanks, General Authority Emeritus, shared the story of a couple who were talking with friends about taking family vacations.

> "It's funny," he said. "We live in an old-fashioned house—legs on the tub, that sort of thing. For years we've been saving up to have the bathroom done over. But every winter we take the money out of the bank and go on a couple of family skiing trips. Our oldest boy is in the army now, and he often mentions in his letters what a great time we had on those trips. You know, I can't imagine his writing home, 'Boy, we really have a swell bathroom, haven't we?'"[21]

And, in the words of President Ezra Taft Benson, "Successful families do things together: family projects, work, vacations, recreation, and reunions."[22]

Conclusion

Elder Henry B. Eyring commented on the promise given in paragraph 7 of the Proclamation.

> The Proclamation is careful in what it promises: "Happiness in family life is most likely to be achieved when founded upon the teachings of the Lord Jesus Christ." My heart aches a little to know that many who read those words will be surrounded by those who do not know or who deny the teachings of Jesus Christ. They can only do their best. But, they can know this: their placement in a family, however challenging, is known by a loving Heavenly Father. They can know that a way is prepared for them to do all that will be required for

them to qualify for eternal life. They may not see how God could give them that gift, nor with whom they will share it. Yet the promise of the gospel of Jesus Christ is sure: "But learn that he who doeth the works of righteousness shall receive his reward, even peace in this world, and eternal life in the world to come. I, the Lord, have spoken it, and the Spirit beareth record. Amen" (D&C 59:23–24).[23]

President Ezra Taft Benson concludes, "Every family has problems and challenges. But successful families try to work together toward solutions instead of resorting to criticism and contention. They pray for each other, discuss, and give encouragement. Occasionally these families fast together in support of one of the family members."[24]

Questions for Thought and Discussion

1. How would you prioritize these nine foundation stones? Which ones do you feel are the most important? Why? What about your potential marriage partner?

2. Use the following questions relative to the nine granite stones, and review how each can be applied to your dating relationships or with the one you intend to marry.

   - Faith in Jesus Christ: How can faith in Jesus Christ strengthen friendships and marriages?

   - Prayer: How could prayer assist you as you prepare for a date? Discuss with someone you are serious about how prayer might strengthen your relationship.

   - Repentance: Are their aspects in your relationships that you need to repent of?

   - Forgiveness: Do you forgive others or do you hold grudges?

   - Respect: Are you respectful of the feelings of others? Do you keep confidences and avoid gossiping?

   - Love: Are you kind in the way you talk to and treat others?

   - Compassion: Do you sincerely listen to others or do most conversations revolve around you?

- Work: Do you enjoy helping others with their projects and activities?

- Wholesome Recreational Activities: Have you determined what activities are appropriate for you to participate in? Do you have the courage to say "no"? Do you need to make any changes in your dating activities?

Suggested Reading

Gordon B. Hinckley, *Ensign*, May 1990, 68.

Neal A. Maxwell, "Put Your Shoulder to the Wheel," *Ensign*, May 1998, 37.

Chapter 16
What Kind of Father Will He Be?

Paragraph 7: By divine design, fathers are to preside over their families in love and righteousness and are responsible to provide the necessities of life and protection for their families.

Introduction

The way you have been parented will have an influence on how you look at fatherhood. This statement from the Proclamation will assist you with understanding what the Lord expects of fathers. As you study this chapter, look for characteristics you would like to have as a future father—or the characteristics you would like in the future father of your children.

A Personal Priesthood Interview

President David O. McKay, said,

> Let me assure you brethren, that someday you will have a personal priesthood interview with the Savior Himself. If you are interested, I will tell you the order in which He will ask you to account for your earthly responsibilities. First: He will request an accountability report about your relationship with your wife. Have you actively been engaged in making her happy and ensuring that her needs have been met as an individual? Second: He will want an accountability report about each of your children individually.[1]

While the world we live in questions the roles of men and women, the Proclamation states very clearly that God has a divine design for fathers and mothers. What is God's design for fathers? Let's call them the three Ps:

- Preside over their families in love and righteousness.

- Provide the necessities of life.

- Protect their families.

A Father Presides in Love and Righteousness

The word *preside* refers to a father's role of leadership in his family. Elder L. Tom Perry of the Quorum of the Twelve Apostles quoted the following from the pamphlet entitled *Father, Consider Your Ways: A Message from The Church of Jesus Christ of Latter-day Saints,*

> Fatherhood is leadership, the most important kind of leadership. It has always been so; it always will be so. Father, with the assistance and counsel and encouragement of your eternal companion, you preside in the home. It is not a matter of whether you are most worthy or best qualified, but it is a matter of [divine] appointment. . . .
>
> You preside at the meal table, at family prayer. You preside at family home evening; and as guided by the Spirit of the Lord, you see that your children are taught correct principles. It is your place to give direction relating to all of family life.
>
> You give father's blessings. You take an active part in establishing family rules and discipline. As a leader in your home you plan and sacrifice to achieve the blessing of a unified and happy family. To do all of this requires that you live a family-centered life.[2]

The Prophet Joseph Smith presided in his home. John Taylor recalled the Prophet teaching him this principle: "It is right for heads of families to get their families together every morning and evening, and pray with them."[3] Orson Pratt saw the Prophet "leading his family in morning and evening devotionals, where 'the words of eternal life flow[ed] from [the Prophet's] lips,' words that were 'nourishing and soothing and comforting [to] his family.'"[4]

Every young man should read and study Doctrine and Covenants 121:34–46. These verses describe a priesthood man as one who presides in love, respect, kindness, and righteousness. A man who dictates orders to his wife and children is not honoring the priesthood he bears.

A Father Provides the Necessities of Life

President Ezra Taft Benson stated what the responsibility of providing life's necessities includes:

> The Lord has charged men with the responsibility to provide for their families in such a way that the wife is allowed to fulfill her role as mother in the home. . . . But we know that sometimes the mother works outside of the home at the encouragement, or even insistence, of her husband . . . [for the] convenience[s] that the extra income can buy. Not only will the family suffer in such instances, brethren, but your own spiritual growth and progression will be hampered.[5]

Joseph Smith, throughout his life, was a hard worker, constantly doing what he could to support his family. This was very difficult for him due to his calling as the Prophet. Through him the Lord said, "Women have claim on their husbands for their maintenance" (D&C 83:2).[6]

To women who, out of necessity, must work, President Gordon B. Hinckley said, "Do the best you can, and remember that the greatest asset you have in this world is those children, whom you've brought into this world, and for whose nurture and care you are responsible."[7]

A Father Protects His Family

What type of protection is the Proclamation referring to? Surely, the Proclamation is referring to both physical and spiritual protection. How does a father provide physical protection? He ensures that his children are taught how to avoid physical harm and injury and he is constantly aware of where his children are, whom they are with, and what activities they are involved in.

And how does he protect them spiritually? He teaches them how to avoid the evils of our day and is an example to his children of what he teaches. He also leads in family prayer, scripture study, and family home evening.

The Prophet Joseph Smith taught, "There is one principle which is eternal; it is the duty of all men to protect their lives and the lives of their household, whenever necessity requires, and no power has a right to forbid it."[8]

Conclusion

I am truly thankful for the opportunity I have been given to be a husband, father, grandfather, and great-grandfather. These callings are great responsibilities and have given me greater joy and even sorrow than I could have ever imagined.

Questions for Thought and Discussion

To Men:

1. What are you doing to prepare yourself to *preside over, provide for*, and *protect* your future wife and family? The type of husband and father you will be is influenced by many of the decisions you are making right now.

2. Are you seeking a vocation that will allow you to spend adequate time with your family?

3. What is your relationship like with your mother? Do you honor and respect her? Do you respect women in general?

4. What qualities would your future marriage partner like in the father of her children? Discuss this with her.

To Women:

1. What type of husband and father are you looking for? One of the ways to determine what type of father he might be is to watch how his father treats his family. Does he *preside, provide,* and *protect*?

2. What is his relationship like with his mother? To determine how he might treat you, watch how he relates with and treats his mother.

3. Discuss with the man you are considering as a husband what he thinks it means to be a good husband and father. Do his answers square with what the Lord has indicated a husband and father should be?

4. Do you respect the men in your life, particularly those who honor the priesthood?

5. Is he on a path that will help him to provide for a family?

6. Is he a hard worker?

7. Now, consider this statement by Elder Richard G. Scott of the Quorum of the Twelve. Does your possible marriage partner show potential as opposed to your image of perfection?

> I suggest that you not ignore many possible candidates [for marriage] who are still developing these attributes. . . . You will not likely find that perfect person, and if you did, there would certainly be no interest in you. These attributes are best polished together as husband and wife.[9]

Suggested Readings

Ezra Taft Benson, "To the Fathers in Israel," *Ensign,* Nov. 1987, 49.

Gordon B. Hinckley, "Our Solemn Responsibilities," *Ensign*, Nov. 1991, 48.

Chapter 17
What Kind of Mother Will She Be?

Paragraph 7: Mothers are primarily responsible for the nurture of their children.

Introduction

Think for a moment about the women who have influenced your life such as your mother, grandmother, sister, aunt, or even cousin. For me, it was my Aunt Helen, who was like a mother to me during my younger years.

When President Gordon B. Hinckley introduced the Proclamation at the 1995 general Relief Society meeting, he said to the women of the Church, "You are the guardians of the hearth. You are the bearers of the children. You are they who nurture them and establish within them the habits of their lives. No other work reaches so close to divinity as does the nurturing of the sons and daughters of God."[1]

President David O. McKay added, "There is nothing so sacred as true womanhood."[2]

The Divine Calling of Mothers Is Being Attacked

As you are likely aware, the divine role of women has been attacked and ridiculed in our society. President Boyd K. Packer referred to this in a talk he gave in April 1964, during a general conference.

> There is a trend in the world today—and unfortunately in the Church—for women to want to be emancipated. And we wonder at times—emancipated from what? From domesticity? From motherhood? From happiness? And to what are you in slavery? Your

children? It is neither necessary nor desirable for the mother of little children to become a drudge or to be relegated to a position of servitude. It is not, however, uncommon to see women—interestingly enough many in the financially well-to-do category—over-surfeiting themselves with activities outside of the home at the expense of their little children. . . . Mothers, do not abandon your responsibilities! Be reverently grateful for your little children.[3]

When we look at the plan of salvation and our divine destiny, doesn't it make sense that the caring and nurturing of Heavenly Father's spirit children would be of supreme importance? The First Presidency of the Church, in 1942, stressed how important mothers are to our Heavenly Father: "Motherhood is near to divinity. It is the highest, holiest service to be assumed by mankind. It places her who honors its holy calling and service next to the angels."[4]

The Divine Pattern

God's divine pattern for women was established when Adam and Eve were cast out of the Garden of Eden. Adam was told he was to earn his bread by the sweat of his brow. (See Genesis 3:19.) To Eve the Lord said that in sorrow she would bring forth children (Genesis 3:16). After Adam and Eve had partaken of the fruit of the tree of knowledge, Eve rejoiced in the opportunity she had to bring children into this world. She said, "Were it not for our transgression we never would have had seed, and never should have known good and evil, and the joy of our redemption, and the eternal life which God giveth unto all the obedient" (Moses 5:11). Eve understood her divine calling as a mother.

President David O. McKay taught that mothers are co-partners with God. "This ability and willingness properly to rear children, the gift to love, and eagerness, yes, longing to express it in soul development, make motherhood the noblest office or calling in the world. . . . In her high duty and service to humanity, endowing with immortality eternal spirits, [a mother] is co-partner with the Creator Himself."[5]

Mothers Have a Gift for Nurturing

The Proclamation states that "mothers are primarily responsible for the nurturing of their children." What does it mean to nurture? Elder M. Russell Ballard said,

Nurturing refers to parenting behaviors such as warmth, support, bonding, attachment, recognizing each child's unique needs and abilities, and attending to children's needs. Nurturing in and of itself is more important in the development of a child than is any particular method or technique of child rearing. It hardly needs saying that nurturing is best carried out in a stable, safe family context.[6]

There are at least two reasons why the Proclamation states that mothers are primarily responsible for the nurturing of children. First, fathers have three responsibilities as discussed in the previous chapter: preside, provide, and protect. This can keep fathers quite busy. Second, mothers have a special gift from our Heavenly Father for loving and nurturing. Elder Neal A. Maxwell, said of his wife Colleen, "Her spiritual antenna on Christian service was always more attuned than mine. So I learned to pay attention over the years when she had those impressions and feelings."[7]

Children Need Their Mothers

In the book *Helping and Healing Our Families*, published by the School of Family Life at BYU, two family researchers have written, "Recent large-scale research found that for young children, more time spent in out-of-home child care arrangements (regardless of quality) is associated with elevated risk for oppositional, disobedient, and aggressive behavior."[8]

Elder Neal A. Maxwell again emphasized the important calling of women:

When the real history of mankind is fully disclosed, will it feature the echoes of gunfire or the shaping sound of lullabies? The great armistices made by military men or the peacemaking of women in homes and neighborhoods? Will what happened in cradles and kitchens prove to be more controlling than what happened in congresses? When the surf of the centuries has made the great pyramids so much sand, the everlasting family will still be standing, because it is a celestial institution, formed outside telestial time.[9]

Motherhood Requires Great Sacrifice

One of the qualities I saw in my wife before we were married was her desire to serve others, and that was one of the primary reasons I loved to be with her. During our marriage, the Lord has blessed us with five children. I have watched her love and mother our children, and I have come to realize the great sacrifices she has made in this divine calling.

President Boyd K. Packer has referred to the sacrifice both husbands and wives make for the children: "A motherly, womanly mother, with her husband, has held a little child in her arms and felt 'here is someone we love more than we love ourselves, here is someone for whom we will do things we never would do for ourselves, and more important than this, here is someone for whom we will give up and cease to do things that we would not otherwise give up and cease doing for ourselves.'"[10]

What about Mothers Working Outside the Home?

On this increasingly prominent topic and debate, President Gordon B. Hinckley has said,

> I think the nurture and upbringing of children is more than a part-time responsibility. I recognize that some women must work, but I fear that there are far too many who do so only to get the means for a little more luxury and a few fancier toys. If you must work, you have an increased load to bear. You cannot afford to neglect your children. They need your supervision in studying, in working inside and outside the home, in the nurturing that only you can adequately give—the love, the blessing, the encouragement, and the closeness of a mother.[11]

Why then has President Gordon B. Hinckley encouraged women to get an education? President Brigham Young is purported to have said the following: "If we educate a man, we educate an individual, but if we educate a woman, we educate a nation."

Conclusion

I have a truly great love, respect, and admiration for the women in my life, especially my dear wife, who has loved and supported me throughout the years and been the mother of our children. I am grateful for the Proclamation and its inspired doctrine, which has taught me both the importance of motherhood and my calling as a husband and father.

Questions for Thought and Discussion

To Men:

1. As you prepare for marriage, are you considering what type of mother you would like your future wife to be?

2. Does the type of a mother she will be rank as high or even higher than physical appearance?

3. Have you taken time to see how your future wife treats young children and what type of a mother her mother is?

To Women:

1. How do you feel about your primary calling of being a wife and mother?

2. What are you doing now to prepare for motherhood?

3. What type of father will your future husband be?

4. Can you stand up against the ways of the world and realize the divine calling you may one day have as a mother?

5. What qualities would your future marriage partner like in you, the woman who may one day be a mother?

Suggested Reading

Spencer W. Kimball, "The Role of Righteous Women," *Ensign*, Nov. 1979, 102.

Chapter 18
Becoming Equal Partners

Paragraph 7: In these sacred responsibilities, fathers and mothers are obligated to help one another as equal partners.

Introduction

Over the centuries since the creation of the earth, many women have been taken advantage of and abused by men. This has happened, in part, because of a false understanding of the importance of womanhood, as shown by how the world has twisted the story of Adam and Eve. Latter-day Saint doctrine looks at the Fall differently. We believe that the Fall was purposeful and Adam and Eve did what they needed to do. We do not look upon it as a sin. Indeed, "Adam fell [and Eve] that man might be. And men are that they might have joy" (2 Nephi 2:25). President Gordon B. Hinckley has said, referring to Genesis 3:16, where it is written that Adam should rule over Eve, "I regrettably recognize that some men have used this through centuries of time as justification for abusing and demeaning women. But . . . in so doing they have demeaned themselves and offended the Father of us all." He then interpreted this scripture to mean that "the husband shall have a governing responsibility to provide for, to protect, to strengthen and shield the wife."[1]

Adam and Eve are an example of being equal partners. Moses 5:1 reads, "And it came to pass that after I, the Lord God, had driven them out, that Adam began to till the earth, and to have dominion over all the beasts of the field, and to eat his bread by the sweat of his brow, as I the Lord had commanded him. And Eve, also, his wife, did labor with him."

Men and women in the Church do not have any basis for the belief that men are better than women. As the Proclamation states, "[We] are obligated to help one another as *equal partners*" (italics added).

What Does It Mean to Be Equal?

President Howard W. Hunter: "Presiding in righteousness necessitates a shared responsibility between husband and wife; together you act with knowledge and participation in all family matters. For a man to operate independent of or without regard to the feelings and the counsel of his wife in governing the family is to exercise unrighteous dominion."[2]

President Gordon B. Hinckley: "In this Church the man neither walks ahead of his wife nor behind his wife but at her side. They are co-equals."[3]

Why This Doctrine Is Important for You

The above statements from our Church leaders describe "equal partners" as both a belief and a behavior. What we sincerely believe in our mind and heart will, to a great degree, influence how we treat our eternal companion. Men or women who feel that they are better than their partner will find it difficult to establish equality in marriage. President Howard W. Hunter, in the quote above, referred to men who exercise "unrighteous dominion" over their wives. This is exemplified by a man who thinks, *I hold the priesthood so she has to do what I say.* Or a man who makes critical decisions for the family without counseling with his wife. Remember, husband and wife should be one in purpose.

Women may also treat their husbands in a condescending and haughty manner, thus destroying any sense of equality in the marriage. A woman might say to her husband, "You hold the priesthood, so get up and do something!" Or she might frequently remind him of mistakes he has made and therefore make decisions without counseling with him.

Treating each other without respect and a sense of equality breeds conflict in marriages. We need to try and understand our partners and their feelings and differing responsibilities. President Ezra Taft Benson said, "There is no inequality between the sexes in God's plan. It is a matter of division of responsibility."[4]

How Is Equality Nurtured in a Marital Relationship?

All marriages require adjustments, repentance, and forgiveness. After all, two imperfect people with different backgrounds and different expectations are coming together with the goal of living together in peace and harmony forever. Such a goal requires time and that they work together as a team. The following ideas come from my relationship with my wife Susan. In the beginning, we faced a number of challenges, mainly because I was not as prepared for marriage as Susan was. But over years of trying to apply the following, we have achieved a level of oneness I never would have imagined possible.

- Each partner in the marriage values and respects the other as a son or daughter of God, with the potential to one day inherit exaltation.

- They pray daily together and each prays consistently for the other, asking Heavenly Father for help in becoming a better partner.

- They show their children how much they love each other.

- They ask for forgiveness often when saying or doing something that hurts the other.

- Regular couple councils are held to discuss family decisions that need to be made relative to children, financial expenses, and how they are each feeling. Each listens to the other, makes suggestions, and come to mutual decisions.

- They share the responsibilities in the home and for teaching their children.

- Each respects the other's freedom to make choices to grow and progress.

- They weather the storms of life, holding tightly to each other and to the covenants they have made with the Savior.

- They attend the temple together frequently to draw closer to the Lord and to each other.

- They have regular dates nights to keep the lines of communication open.

Conclusion

President Thomas S. Monson has encouraged both men and women to accept the responsibility of creating love and unity in their marriage. "Brethren, let's treat our wives with dignity and respect. They're our eternal companions. Sisters, honor your husbands. They need to hear a good word. They need a friendly smile. They need a warm expression of true love."[5]

Perhaps one of the finest examples of what it means to be equal partners in marriage is President Gordon B. Hinckley. In an interview, Sister Hinckley shared the following about her husband: "Gordon always let me do my own thing. He never insisted that I do anything his way or any way for that matter. From the beginning he gave me space and let me fly."[6]

Questions for Thought and Discussion

1. Do you respect and value the opposite sex?

2. What have you learned from your own family about what it means to be equal partners?

3. Are there things you would like to do differently than your parents did?

4. Discuss together what it means to be an equal partner. How will you ensure that you are equal partners in your marriage?

5. When dating, are you treated respectfully by those you date?

Suggested Readings

Ensign, November 1978, 106.

Elder Bruce C. Hafen, "Crossing the Thresholds and Becoming Equal Partners," *Ensign*, August 2007.

Chapter 19
Dealing with the Unexpected

Paragraph 7: Disability, death, or other circumstances may necessitate individual adaptation. Extended families should lend support when needed.

Introduction

The end of paragraph 7 of the Proclamation—after presenting important principles that successful marriages and families are based on—states that there are circumstances where adaptation may be required. In a perfect world, all marriages would be happy, all children would be obedient, and all major challenges (like those mentioned in the Proclamation) would not happen. The prophets and apostles who gave us this inspired Proclamation recognized that we live in an imperfect world with imperfect people.

Of course, adapting to changing circumstances may not always be easy. Most of us do not like change; we want to stay in a lifestyle that we are used to and comfortable with. In Church history, there are a number of examples of the Lord asking the saints to adapt to change. Missouri was to be the place where Zion would be redeemed, but enemies of the Church combined to drive the Saints out. Talk about adapting! A swamp area in Illinois with mosquitoes and diseases had to be adapted to. But the Saints have always had the ability to change and meet whatever circumstances they found themselves in. Today is no different. As the Proclamation states: "Disability, death, or other circumstances may necessitate individual adaptation." Sometimes roles might need to be reversed. A father may need to assume a greater role in household duties and the nurturing of children should his wife become ill. A full-time mother may need to enter the workforce if her husband becomes ill or loses his job. The death of a spouse certainly would change the dynamics of a family. Also, divorce would require both parties to have to adapt to their new circumstance.

What to Do When These Unforeseen Issues Arise?

The Proclamation offers the Lord's solution when adapting is required: "Extended families should lend support where needed."

Elder L. Tom Perry said, "To build a foundation strong enough to support a family in our troubled world today requires the best effort of each of us—father, mother, brother, sister, grandmother, grandfather, aunts, uncles, cousins, and so on. Each must contribute energy and effort in driving piles right down to the bedrock of the gospel until the foundation is strong enough to endure through the eternities."[1]

To accomplish what Elder Perry said requires the love, sacrifice, and patience of every family member. For instance, say the parents of a family of four children found out that their youngest daughter had cancer. This would require many medical visits with long hours of chemotherapy, leaving their other three children at home. But then grandmother came to the rescue. She would have to leave her husband and life for a number of weeks so she could be with the three grandchildren to love and nurture them. This required a sacrifice on the part of the grandparents, but isn't that what families are for?

I have seen this type of support when my wife and I served our mission in India. When something happened to a member of the family, all the extended family came to the aid of that person.

Conclusion

I assure you that in your future you will have many opportunities to adapt to changing circumstances. This will be a blessing for you as you prepare to one day marry. Learn now to adapt to change with patience, self-control, and faith in the Lord that things will work out.

Questions for Thought and Discussion

1. What kind of support might either of you receive from your extended family if there were a problem?

2. Are you comfortable with each other's parents? Remember, when you marry you also marry into the other's family.

3. What will you do to establish your own family separate from your parents?

4. What experiences have you had that required you to adapt through sacrifice and patience?

Chapter 20
A Warning and an Invitation

Paragraphs 8 and 9: We warn that individuals who violate covenants of chastity, who abuse spouse or offspring, or who fail to fulfill family responsibilities will one day stand accountable before God. Further, we warn that the disintegration of the family will bring upon individual, communities, and nations the calamities foretold by ancient and modern prophets.

We call upon responsible citizens and officers of government everywhere to promote those measures designed to maintain and strengthen the family as the fundamental unit of society.

Introduction

One of the responsibilities of prophets in any dispensation is to teach the doctrines and principles that assist people in walking the path back to the Lord. Prophets also warn us of impending danger. The Lord has said, "And the voice of warning shall be unto all people, by the mouths of my disciples, whom I have chosen in these last days" (D&C 1:4).

The scriptures are a witness that the words of the prophets are always fulfilled:

> What I the Lord have spoken, I have spoken, and I excuse not myself; and though the heavens and the earth pass away, my word shall not pass away, but shall all be fulfilled, whether by mine own voice or the voice of my servants, it is the same (D&C 1:38).

In the Proclamation, the prophets have warned that the way you treat your baptismal and temple covenants will determine the blessings you receive now and where you will be in the eternities. They have reminded you that chastity before and fidelity after marriage is a commandment of God. You have also been counseled about the importance of marriage and family. The type of husband or wife you become will determine much of your happiness now and in the future.

Abuse in any form is not tolerated by the Lord. The First Presidency has said, "Abuse is the physical, emotional, sexual, or spiritual mistreatment of others. It may not only harm the body, but it can deeply affect the mind and spirit, destroying faith and causing confusion, doubt, mistrust, guilt, and fear."[1]

You must study and connect with the Proclamation for it to have meaning in your life. As you are probably not married, it will not be good enough for you to wait until you are married to apply the principles you have read. Between now and then, you may make mistakes that could affect your future marriage and family. You need to be converted to the principles of the Proclamation now. There is simply too much at stake for you now and in your future.

Prophetic Warnings

The Proclamation concludes with a prophecy: "The disintegration of the family will bring upon individuals, communities, and nations the calamities foretold by ancient and modern prophets." What are some of these calamities?

Doctrine and Covenants 5:19: "For a desolating scourge shall go forth among the inhabitants of the earth, and shall continue to be poured out from time to time, if they repent not, until the earth is empty, and the inhabitants thereof are consumed away and utterly destroyed by the brightness of my coming."

Doctrine and Covenants 109:45: "We know that thou hast spoken by the mouth of thy prophets terrible things concerning the wicked, in the last days—that thou wilt pour out thy judgments, without measure."

Joseph Smith Matthew 1: 29–30: "Behold I speak for mine elect's sake; for nation shall rise against nation, and kingdom against kingdom; there shall be famines, and pestilences, and earthquakes, in divers places. And again, because iniquity shall abound, the love of men shall wax cold; but he that shall not be overcome, the same shall be saved."

Did you notice that all of these prophecies had one thing in common? If the people of the world do not repent, the judgments of God will come, as has been said since the world began. This is particularly true in regards to those who have made covenants with the Lord in baptism and in the temple.

Of what does the world need to repent? Answer: all of the efforts to demean and attack the traditional family. Remember, if Elijah had not come, the earth would have been utterly wasted at the Lord's coming. This reminds us that, to God, the family is of utmost importance. It is why He created this earth! Efforts made by politicians and political groups to undermine the family will end in disaster.

Holding Up the Proclamation

Julie B. Beck, former General President of the Relief Society, said, "This generation will be called upon to defend the doctrine of the family as never before."[2]

What can you do to promote and defend the teachings of the Proclamation? Elder M. Russell Ballard has asked us to hold it up as a banner:

> Brothers and sisters, as we hold up like a banner the proclamation to the world on the family and as we live and teach the gospel of Jesus Christ, we will fulfill the measure of our creation here on earth. We will find peace and happiness here and in the world to come. We should not need a hurricane or other crisis to remind us of what matters most. The gospel and the Lord's plan of happiness and salvation should remind us. What matters most is what lasts longest, and our families are for eternity.[3]

President Gordon B. Hinckley added, "The Proclamation on the Family is a wonderful statement, but I want to say this, it will mean absolutely nothing unless we bring its principles into our lives."[4]

Conclusion

How can you hold up the Proclamation like a banner?

- Live the teachings contained in it. Be an example to those around you of what the Proclamation teaches.

- Share it with friends and family and let them know you believe it to be the word of God.

- Share your testimony that the principles therein are true.

- Let local politicians know of your feelings about the family and that you oppose any efforts to change its traditional structure.

- When you hear people say negative things about marriage and family, stand up and defend the principles in the Proclamation.

- Make the principles in the Proclamation the focus of your dating life.

- When you feel you have met someone who you might want to marry, review the Proclamation word by word and discuss how you feel about each principle.

One day, you will stand before Heavenly Father to give an account of your mission in mortality. He could well ask you what you did to live and promote the doctrines and principles in this inspired Proclamation. It explicitly says that you and I "will one day stand accountable before God."

Suggested Reading

Elder Richard G. Scott, "Healing the Tragic Scars of Abuse," *Ensign*, May 1992.

Appendix
Seven Suggestions for Choosing
Your Eternal Companion

So as you are likely aware of at this point, marriage is one of the biggest decisions you will ever make in your life. Perhaps you have wondered why the Lord has not given you more help in making this decision. Some people want a direct sign like a bolt of lightning or having Moroni drop the gold plates on their head. That is usually not the way Heavenly Father works. This is an area where He has given you agency to choose. Of course, He will help you, but you are expected to make the decision.

Oliver Cowdery, one of the scribes of the Book of Mormon, learned this lesson the hard way. He wanted to translate the sacred record and so the Lord allowed him to do so. But he failed, and the Lord said to him,

> Behold, you have not understood; you have supposed that I would give it unto you, when you took no thought save it was to ask me. But behold, I say unto you, that you must study it out in your mind; then you must ask me if it be right (D&C 9:8).

Applying the principle in this scripture to your life, the decision of whom you should marry begins first with you. Here are seven suggestions to assist you.

Make Friends with the Opposite Sex

The more friends you have of the opposite sex, the more opportunity you will have to discover the type of person you would be most compatible with. That is the major purpose of dating. This is one of the reasons Church leaders have counseled youth to avoid steady dating until the boy has served a mission or the young woman is past her teenage years. You may have heard of the "vanilla theory," which is if you only eat vanilla ice cream you will never appreciate chocolate, strawberry, raspberry, and so on.

If you are shy or reserved, you will need to get outside your comfort zone and attend activities where you will meet more people. You might also need to learn some social skills so that you can get to know others. When I was teaching institute at a university, a young man came to me and asked how he could learn to talk with girls. He was from a small farming community and had never dated during high school. When he arrived at the university, he enrolled in a dance class to try and meet some girls. During one of the classes, the male students were given a free dance where they could ask someone to dance. He chose a girl and, as they danced, his mind went totally blank. He could not think of anything to talk about. After the dance, he was really embarrassed and couldn't look the girl in the face from then on.

I suggested that he write scripts, like a person would do for a play. "Write down different questions you could ask a girl to get to know her," I said. So he did just that. Some of the questions were, "What hobbies do you have?" "What are some of your favorite school subjects?" "Why do you like that subject the best?" He wrote a number of these down and memorized them. He said that as he practiced asking girls questions, he learned a lot and began to feel more at ease.

Look for More than Just Physical Appearance

I had an experience a number of years ago that has really stuck with me. I was walking down the halls of a busy university when a group of boys walked past me. As girls walked past, I heard the boys say to each other, "She's a five, she's an eight, and she's a ten." I thought, *Boys will be boys.* But then I realized that our society is bombarded with the message that physical attraction is the most important thing in a relationship. People are conditioned to think this by movies, music, television, and your friends. *He (or she) is hot* is the message that you hear all of the time. While physical attraction is important in marriage, it is only one of many important characteristics. You are not just marrying a physical body. You marry a person who has habits, desires, and faults of which you may not be aware.

Another problem with placing physical attraction as the number one priority is that many wonderful people may be passed by in dating because they might not be an eight or a ten. Such things as compatible values, good temperament, and a service-oriented mentality are critical to a happy marriage. I believe that one of the reasons for the growing divorce rate among members of the Church is that physical attraction is, in many cases, the most important (or the most immediate) priority, and couples do not take time to look for other qualities.

Give Yourself the Opportunity to Mature and Find out about Yourself to Become the Right One

This generation is said to be the "coddled generation." This is a time of unprecedented wealth and materialism. Many have been raised getting everything they want without learning to work or sacrifice. While most enter marriage not as prepared as they should be, some marry totally unprepared for the demands and sacrifices that will be required.

Prophets have identified selfishness as the number one cause of divorce among Church members. A mature person is able to postpone personal wants and desires for the benefit of others.

So how do you develop the maturity that will prepare you for marriage? Here are some suggestions:

- Get a part-time or full-time job so you learn how to work.

- Learn to get along with roommates. Immaturity is often found between roommates. As an institute director, one of the most common problems I dealt with was roommate issues.

- Serve a full mission. A mission, possibly more than any other activity, will prepare you for marriage.

- Quit texting or playing video games so much. Read some books about preparing for marriage, Church-issued or otherwise.

- Establish a financial budget for yourself so that you learn to manage money. Money can be a huge wedge in a marriage. Learn the difference between wants and needs.

- Make a sincere effort to control your emotions. Anger, jealousy, and depressive disorders can destroy a marriage very quickly. If you have a serious problem with any of these, see your bishop and get a recommendation from him for a good counselor or medical doctor. Do this before you are married.

Perhaps you might think that this suggestion is foolish and doesn't apply to you. But the more mature and emotionally stable you are, the better chance you will have of enjoying a happy marriage. The same thing applies to the person you feel you are in love with.

Some people write a list of things they want in a future mate. Elder Bednar has referred to this as "a shopping list," which, he said, is arrogant and egotistical.[1] I have learned that there is a principle called the "law of attraction." In the Doctrine and Covenants 88:40, the Lord said, "For intelligence cleaveth unto intelligence; wisdom receiveth wisdom; truth embraceth truth; virtue loveth virtue." This law indicates that we will attract the type of person we are. So, if you make a list of the qualities you want in a companion, begin working to acquire those qualities in your life. You will attract the type of person you are.

Don't Rush into Marriage

Sometimes members of the Church feel immense pressure to marry. This often comes from parents or other members. You must not make the mistake of marrying just to please others. You must also be careful not to postpone marriage. As you are aware, the doctrine of the gospel teaches us that a happy marriage is essential to inheriting the highest degree of the celestial kingdom. Therefore, we should be preparing to marry the right person in the right place.

Another way you might be pressured to marry is if the one you are currently dating says, "The Lord has revealed to me that you should marry me." When it comes to the marriage decision (or any personal revelation), no one else has the right to revelation for you, not even your possible future spouse.

One of the most important things you will do to prepare for marriage is getting to know the person you are considering marrying. Because love is such a powerful emotion, couples often marry on emotion rather than actually evaluating the relationship rationally. Strong emotion usually shoves rational thinking right out the window!

Here is a challenge many couples face during the courtship process. During this time, we often put on our best face to impress the other person. We do not want our date to see our real side. I call this "the moon effect." The moon has a dark side and a light side, but we never see the dark side. If you are not careful and rush into marriage, you might not really know whom you are marrying. One woman said to me, "The person I thought I was marrying and the person I actually married were two different people. I had no idea how controlling and manipulative he was." Another said, "My marriage was like taking a flight to New York and when I landed I found out I was in Pittsburgh." Why didn't they figure this out before they married? They allowed emotion to override their thinking processes. I am not suggesting here that feelings of the heart are not important, but there must be a balance between the heart and the mind. If I were asked which was the most important, I would lean strongly to the rational side.

The Lord told Oliver Cowdery "to study" the problem "out in his mind." That is wonderful counsel for someone preparing for marriage. How do you "study" a relationship out in your mind? You do things that help you see the real person you think you are in love with. Here are some suggestions:

- Do activities with his or her family. See how the parents treat each other and how he or she treats his or her parents. The young man will often have many traits like his father and the young woman will often have many traits like her mother, though this can vary.

- Once you both feel you are in love, discuss important values together. How do you both feel about the gospel? What do you feel are the roles of husband and wife? What are your views about having and raising children? Are you compatible socially? That is, do you have activities that you enjoy doing together?

- Volunteer to babysit children together. How does the other interact with them? How well do you get along together with children?

- Read the Proclamation together. Discuss each sentence and share how you feel about the counsel given. I believe that this is the single most important activity a couple can do together. The Proclamation is the best description of what Heavenly Father feels we need to know about marriage and family.

- You might also consider going on the BYU website and, for a small fee, take the compatibility questionnaire called RELATE. This was developed by Latter-day Saint marriage and family teachers.

An LDS marriage counselor told me that one of the major problems he had seen in marriages was spouses thinking they can change the other person after they have gotten married. He said, "This is simply not true! What you see is usually what you get." Therefore, you need to take time to get to know the person you want to marry.

Do Not Let Physical Intimacy Cloud Your Judgment and Destroy Your Relationship

When physical intimacy enters into the relationship, a number of dangerous things start to happen. I am talking here about too much passionate kissing, touching private places on each other's bodies, and sexual relations. For most Latter-day Saint couples, this begins slowly and then escalates. You need to be aware of the consequences should you choose to follow the ways of the world:

- You will lose the comforting Spirit of the Holy Ghost to guide your decision-making.

- Your relationship will begin to focus almost entirely on the physical aspect of your relationship that should be saved for marriage. Instead of love, lust will begin to be the focus.

- You will start talking less and emotion will take over rational thinking.

- You will begin to feel guilty and not worthy.

- You will argue more with the one you think you love.

- You will not have the opportunity to marry in the Lord's temple.

- Your respect and trust for each other will begin to fade.

In the book *How Do You Know When You're Really in Love?*, I shared the story of a couple who came to me with a problem. They indicated that they had been dating for a few months and felt they were in love. However, recently they had started to argue and they just didn't feel the close relationship they had felt earlier. I asked them if they had been doing things contrary to the commandments of the Lord. They said that they had. I said that was the problem. The Spirit of the Lord had been pushed out of their relationship and they needed to see their respective bishops as soon as possible.

To avoid these consequences of immorality, you need to establish strict rules to protect your virtue and your future marriage. We learn a great principle in the war section of the Book of Mormon. Amalickiah certainly represents the devil and the Lamanites his host of evil spirits. Their desire was to destroy the Nephites, just as Satan desires to destroy you and your future happiness. To protect his people, Captain Moroni prepared his people for Amalickiah's attacks by putting armor on his soldiers and fortifying their cities. He had mounds of dirt with pickets built on timbers and ditches placed around each city to counter the rocks and arrows of their enemies. You must never forget that the devil is your enemy. You need to do everything you can to protect yourself. Here are ways to prepare:

- Make a commitment to Heavenly Father that you will study the scriptures each day and pray to Him at least at night and in the morning. This will help keep the Spirit active in your life.

- Attend Church—especially sacrament meeting—and renew your promises with the Lord. The sacrament is a time to make sure you are on the path the Lord has outlined. If you have been endowed in the temple, attend often to feel peace and pray. Put a picture of the temple in a place where you can see it every day.

- Keep a kiss sacred. Too much kissing is the place where a loss of virtue begins.

- Never lie down together, even to study or watch a movie.

- Never be in a bedroom together until you are married.

- Avoid watching movies, DVDs, or television programs that promote immoral behavior: living together before marriage, couples in bed together, couples making out, partial nudity. You might say, "Well, that leaves out most movies!" You are absolutely right! But it is worth it to safeguard the precious gift the Lord has given you: your virtue. Before my wife and I watch any movie, we go to *dove.com* and review the content. Many television programs should also be avoided. Whether you realize it or not, you are being conditioned by what you see and hear. Media is the devil's most effective tool to deprive you of happiness in marriage. Remember, he will never be able to marry or have a family. Therefore, he is out to destroy yours.

- Avoid pornography. It is a plague. Pornography is a major problem within the Church. Why else would the leaders of the Church speak so often about it? If you are involved with pornography, you are not at all prepared for marriage. A young man or young woman involved in pornography will have unrealistic and false sexual expectations.

Should you make a mistake and do something you know is unworthy, remember two things: Heavenly Father still loves you and He has given you a bishop who will help you repent and get the Spirit back in your life.

Make a Decision Using Your Best Judgment

This is the challenging part of making the decision to marry or not to marry: the actual decision. You must try and set emotion somewhat aside and use your mental faculties to actually weigh the positive and negative aspects of the relationship. This, it seems to me, is what the Lord means by studying it out in your mind. Remember, if you are physically involved, this will be a difficult thing to do because emotions associated with lust are incredibly strong and binding.

Here is a suggestion to assist you. Use the following chart to evaluate your relationship. Pray as you do this.

	Yes	No
Are you of the same religion?		
Are you totally honest with each other?		
Do you share similar values?		
Have you spent enough time together to really get to know each other?		

Do you have similar friends?		
Do you have similar interests?		
Have you ever had to resolve conflicts together?		
Are your goals similar?		

Seek the Lord's Confirmation of Your Decision

One of the most frequently-asked questions when I was teaching institute was, "How do I distinguish between the Spirit of the Lord and my own emotions?"

Before getting to that, here are three principles to consider:

The Lord's timing. You must be patient when seeking answers. Heavenly Father will answer when He knows it is best.

The line upon line principle. In 2 Nephi 28:30, the Lord gives this insight to Nephi, "For behold, thus saith the Lord God: I will give unto the children of men line upon line, precept upon precept, here a little and there a little."

I have talked with some Church members who believe that revelation should come instantly or as they were praying about whom to marry. Note how Elder Bednar came to know he should marry his wife.

> Sister Bednar and I knew each other for 19 months and dated for 15 months before we were married. I do not recall ever receiving a single, overwhelming spiritual confirmation that she was "the one." I do recall that as we dated, as we talked, as we became better acquainted, and as we observed and learned about each other in a variety of circumstances, I received many small, simple, and quiet reassurances that she was indeed a remarkable and spiritual woman. All of those simple answers over a period of time led to and produced an appropriate spiritual reassurance that indeed we were to be married. That reassurance did not come all at once; rather, it was spiritually subtle and gradually distilled upon our minds as the dews from heaven, as described in the 121st section of the Doctrine and Covenants (see verse 45).[2]

Elder Bednar's experience teaches some important principles about knowing whom to marry:

- They did not rush into marriage because of a strong emotional feeling.

- They dated for a time to allow them to get to know each other and allow the Spirit of the Lord to gradually work on them.

- The reassurance that they were to marry came over a period of time with small, simple feelings from the Spirit.

- He did not receive a great, overwhelming spiritual experience.

He does indicate later in his talk that he is not saying everyone must follow their pattern. But to those who do not receive a powerful spiritual witness as to whom they are to marry, maybe the Lord is working with them "line upon line, precept upon precept."

The worthiness issue. We must seek to be worthy to receive revelation. This is why, if you become involved with immorality, you will not be in a position to receive the Lord's guidance.

Now, once you have made a decision and are prayerfully requesting confirmation, how do you recognize answers from the Spirit? The scriptures are filled with examples of how revelation comes. In Doctrine and Covenants 8:2, the Lord tells us how revelation is received, "I will tell you in your mind and in your heart, by the Holy Ghost." Here is a summary of what I have found:

- In the heart: calm, peace, light, assurance, comfort, serenity, confidence.

- In the mind: persistent impressions, pressing ideas, a still small voice that whispers.

Certainly we must place ourselves in the right situations to hear God's voice. This could be one reason we have been counseled to pray and ponder in a quiet place, to listen to uplifting music, to attend Sacrament meeting early to listen to the prelude music, and so on. Answers come when we are in the right place doing the right things. Perhaps now if you didn't realize it before, you understand why Church leaders have counseled us to be careful of the places we go, the programs we watch, and the music we listen to.

I hope these suggestions will assist you as you prepare for your eternal marriage.

Endnotes

Chapter 1

1. Gordon B. Hinckley, "Stand Strong Against the Wiles of the World," *Ensign,* Nov. 1995, 100.
2. Hugh B. Brown, "Loyalty to the Church," Conference Report, Oct. 1961, 84–85.
3. Harold B. Lee, "President Lee Speaks," *Church News*, Aug. 19, 1972, 3.
4. Spencer W. Kimball, "Families Can Be Forever," *Ensign,* Nov. 1980, 4.
5. BYU, *Strengthening Our Families*, "The State of American Families."
6. Alexander Pope, *An Essay on Man*, 1734.
7. David O. McKay, *Gospel Ideals*, under "Courtship and Marriage."
8. Spencer W. Kimball, "We Need a Listening Ear," *Ensign*, Nov. 1979.
9. Ezra Taft Benson, *Teachings of Ezra Taft Benson*, Deseret Book, 1988.
10. Howard W. Hunter, "Exceeding Great and Precious Promises," *Ensign*, Nov. 1994.
11. Gordon B. Hinckley, "Standing Strong and Immovable," Worldwide Leadership Training Meeting, Jan. 2004, 21.
12. Joseph Smith, as quoted by John Taylor, *Millennial Star*, Nov. 1851, 339.
13. Satellite Broadcast to the Churches in Southern California, Jan. 2014.

Chapter 2

1. Joseph Smith, *History of the Church*, July 1839, 383.
2. Boyd K. Packer, "For Time and all Eternity," Nov. 1993.
3. Joseph B. Wirthlin, "Journey to Higher Ground," *Ensign*, Nov. 2005.
4. Harold B. Lee, "Uphold the Hands of the President of the Church," *Conference Report*, Oct. 1970, 152.
5. Joseph Fielding Smith, "Eternal Keys and the Right to Preside," *Ensign*, July 1972, 88.
6. Gordon B. Hinckley, "Loyalty," *Ensign*, May 2003, 60.

Chapter 3

1. John and Kimberly Bytheway, *What We Wished We'd Known When We Were Newlyweds.* Salt Lake City: Deseret Book, 2000.

2. Merrill J. Bateman, "The Eternal Family," in *Brigham Young University 1997–98 Speeches* [1997], 115.

3. Gordon B. Hinckley, "The Women in Our Lives," *Ensign*, Nov. 2004, 84.

4. Tad R. Callister, *The Inevitable Apostasy.* Salt Lake City: Deseret Book, 2006.

5. Boyd K. Packer, "For Time and All Eternity," *Ensign*, Nov. 1993.

6. Howard W. Hunter, *Teachings of Howard W. Hunter.* Salt Lake City: Deseret Book, 1997, 140.

7. Thomas S. Monson, "Priesthood Power," *Ensign*, May 2011.

8. Ezra Taft Benson, "To the Single Adults of the Church," *Ensign*, Nov. 1988.

9. Robert D. Hales, "Celestial Marriage: A Little Heaven on Earth," BYU fireside, Nov. 9, 1976.

10. M. Russell Ballard, "What Matters Most Is What Lasts Longest," *Ensign*, Nov. 2005.

11. David A. Bednar, "Marriage Is Essential to His Eternal Plan," *Ensign*, June 2006.

12. Boyd K. Packer, *Mine Errand from the Lord*, Salt Lake City: Deseret Book, 2009, 267.

13. James E. Faust, "Father, Come Home," *Ensign*, May 1993, 36–37.

Chapter 4

1. David A. Bednar, Worldwide Leadership Training, Feb. 2006, 2–3.

2. Hugh B. Brown, *Improvement Era*, December 1966, 1095.

3. Neal A. Maxwell, "The Richness of the Restoration," *Ensign*, Sept. 2001.

4. Brigham Young, *Discourses of Brigham Young*, Salt Lake City: Deseret News Press, 1993, 76–78.

5. Joseph Smith, *Teachings of the Prophet Joseph Smith*, Salt Lake City: Deseret Book, 1976, 181.

6. Joseph Smith, "The King Follett Sermon," *Ensign*, May 1971, 13.

7. Joseph Smith, *Teachings of the Prophet Joseph Smith*, Salt Lake City: Deseret Book, 1976, 357.

8. Ibid., 181.

9. Ibid., 255–256.

10. Dallin H. Oaks, "The Great Plan of Happiness," *Ensign*, Nov. 1993, 72.

11. Ezra Taft Benson, "To the 'Youth of the Noble Birthright,'" *Ensign*, Nov. 1986.

Chapter 5

1. Boyd K. Packer, "Our Moral Environment," *Ensign*, May 1992.
2. BYU, *Strengthening Our Families*, 34.
3. George Q. Cannon, *Gospel Truths*, Comp. Jerald Newquist, 1974.
4. Boyd K. Packer, "To Young Women and Young Men," *Ensign*, May 1987, 54.
5. Thomas S. Monson, "Yellow Canaries With Gray on Their Wings," *Ensign*, July 1973.
6. Gordon B. Hinckley, *Teachings of Gordon B. Hinckley*, Salt Lake City: Deseret Book, 1997, 159.
7. Thomas S. Monson, "Your Patriarchal Blessing," *Ensign*, Feb. 2010.
8. Boyd K. Packer, *Mine Errand from the Lord*, Salt Lake City: Deseret Book, 2009, 209.
9. Dallin H. Oaks, "The Great Plan of Happiness," *Ensign*, Nov. 1993, 72.

Chapter 6

1. Douglas Callister, BYU–Idaho Devotional, March 13, 2012.
2. Joseph Smith, *Teachings of the Presidents of the Church*, Salt Lake City: Deseret Book, 1976, 211.
3. Douglas Callister, BYU–Idaho Devotional, March 13, 2012.
4. Joseph Smith, "The King Follett Sermon," *Ensign*, May 1971, 13.
5. Boyd K. Packer, "The Least of These," *Ensign*, Nov. 2004, 87.
6. Pierre Teilhad de Chardin, as quoted by Carolyn J. Rasmus in *In the Strength of the Lord*. Salt Lake City: Deseret Book, 1990.
7. Lorenzo Snow, *Teachings of the Presidents of the Church*, The Church of Jesus Christ of Latter-day Saints, 84.
8. F. Burton Howard, "Eternal Marriage," *Conference Report*, April 2003.

Chapter 7

1. *Doctrine and Covenants Student Manual*, 2002, 76.
2. Bruce R. McConkie, "Celestial Marriage," BYU Fireside, Nov. 6, 1977.
3. John and Kimberly Bytheway, *What We Wished We'd Known When We Were Newlyweds*. Sal Lake City: Deseret Book, 2000.
4. Parley P. Pratt, *Autobiography of Parley P. Pratt*, 1985, 259–60.
5. Orson F. Whitney, "Latter-day Saint Ideals and Institutions," *Improvement Era*, Aug. 1927, 851.

6. Joseph Smith, *Teachings of the Prophet Joseph Smith*, Salt Lake City: Deseret Book, 1976, 354.

7. Joseph Fielding Smith, *The Restoration of All Things*, Salt Lake City: Deseret News Press, 1945.

8. Henry B. Eyring, "Hearts Bound Together," *Ensign*, May 2005, 78.

9. Brigham Young, *Teachings of the President of the Church*, 164.

10. Gordon B. Hinckley, "Life's Obligations," *Ensign*, Feb. 1999, 2.

11. Boyd K. Packer, *The Holy Temple*. Bookcraft, 1980, 182, 253.

Chapter 8

1. David A. Bednar, "We Believe in Being Chaste," *Ensign*, May 2013, 41.

2. Billy Graham, as quoted by Spencer W. Kimball, "Guidelines to Carry Forth the Word of God in Cleanliness," *Ensign*, May 1974.

3. Boyd K. Packer, *Mine Errand from the Lord*, Salt Lake City: Deseret Book, 2009, 229.

4. Richard G. Scott, "Make the Right Choices," *Ensign*, Nov. 1994, 38.

5. Ezra Taft Benson, *The Teachings of Ezra Taft Benson*, 285.

6. Boyd K. Packer, *Our Father's Plan*. Salt Lake City: Deseret Book, 1994, 27.

7. Spencer W. Kimball, "Talking With Your Children about Moral Purity," *Ensign*, Dec. 1986.

8. Stephen Arterbaum and Fred Stockor, *Everyman's Battle: Winning the War on Sexual Temptation One Victory at a Time*, 2000, 57.

9. Gordon B. Hinckley, "Reverence and Morality," *Ensign*, May 1987.

10. Jeffrey R. Holland, "How Do I Love Thee?" *New Era*, Oct. 2003.

11. Susan Tanner, BYU–Idaho Devotional, "Friendship, Courtship, Physical Relationship," May 18, 2003.

12. Hugh W. Pinnock, "Ten Keys to Successful Dating and Marriage," BYU Fireside, May 3, 1981.

Chapter 9

1. Neal A. Maxwell, "The Inexhaustible Gospel," *Ensign*, Apr. 1993, 68–73.

2. BYU, *Strengthening Our Families*, 207.

3. Church Handbook of Instructions #1, 2010.

4. Gordon B. Hinckley, "Save the Children," *Ensign*, Nov. 1994, 53.

5. Spencer W. Kimball, "Very Much Alive," LDS Church Filmstrip, 1976, Salt Lake City, Utah.

Chapter 10

1. Thomas S. Monson, "Priesthood Power," *Ensign*, May 2011, 66.

2. Boyd K. Packer, *Mine Errand From the Lord*, Salt Lake City: Deseret Book, 2009, 257–58.

3. Dallin H. Oaks, "The Great Plan of Happiness," *Ensign*, Nov. 1993, 75.

4. Julie Beck, "What Latter-day Saint Women Do Best: Stand Strong and Immovable," *Ensign*, Nov. 2007.

5. Dallin H. Oaks, "The Great Plan of Happiness," *Ensign*, Nov. 1993, 75.

6. Encyclopedia of Mormonism, "Birth Control."

7. David O. McKay, *Gospel Ideals*. Salt Lake City: Deseret Book, 1953, 469.

Chapter 11

1. BYU, *Strengthening Our Families*, 35.

2. LDS Bible Dictionary, 632.

3. Gordon B. Hinckley, "Except the Lord Build the House," *Ensign*, June 1971, 71.

4. Richard G. Scott, "Making the Right Choices," *Ensign*, May 1991, 35.

5. Thomas S. Monson, *The Teachings of Thomas S. Monson*, Salt Lake City: Deseret Book, 2011, 174.

6. Marvin J. Ashton, "Love Takes Time," *Ensign*, Nov. 1975.

7. Spencer W. Kimball, *The Miracle of Forgiveness*, Salt Lake City: Deseret Book, 1969, 242.

8. Spencer W. Kimball, *Teachings of Spencer W. Kimball*, Bookcraft, 1995, 279.

9. David O. McKay, *Gospel Ideals*. Salt Lake City: Deseret Book, 1953.

Chapter 12

1. Thomas S. Monson, *The Teachings of Thomas S. Monson*, Salt Lake City: Deseret Book, 2011, 209.

2. James E. Faust, "The Greatest Challenge in the World: Good Parenting," *Ensign*, Nov. 2005, 3.

3. "Proclamation," *Ensign*, May 1980, 52.

4. Gordon B. Hinckley, *Discourses of Gordon B. Hinckley*, Salt Lake City: Deseret Book, 2005, 588.

Chapter 13

1. Spencer W. Kimball, "Ocean Currents and Family Influences," *Ensign*, Nov. 1974, 112.

2. oxforddictionaries.com.

3. Gordon B. Hinckley, "Our Solemn Responsibilities," *Ensign*, Nov. 1991.

4. Spencer W. Kimball, *Teachings of Spencer W. Kimball*, Bookcraft, 1995, 279.

5. Hugh W. Pinnock, "Ten Keys to Successful Dating and Marriage," BYU Fireside May 3, 1981.

6. David B. Haight, "Marriage and Divorce," *Ensign*, May 1984, 14.

Chapter 14

1. Robert D. Hales, "Celestial Marriage: A Little Heaven on Earth," BYU Fireside, Nov. 9, 1976.

2. Howard W. Hunter, "Reading the Scriptures," *Ensign*, Nov. 1979.

3. Hugh W. Pinnock, "Ten Keys to Successful Dating and Marriage," BYU Fireside May 3, 1981.

Chapter 15

1. Brigham Young, "We are building a temple to last . . ."

2. Dallin H. Oaks, "Faith in the Lord Jesus Christ," *Ensign*, May 1994.

3. David B. Haight, "Marriage and Divorce," *Ensign*, May 1984, 14.

4. David A. Bednar, "Pray Always," *Ensign*, Nov. 2008.

5. Ezra Taft Benson, "Counsel to the Saints," *Ensign*, May 1989.

6. Richard G. Scott, *21 Principles*. Salt Lake City: Deseret Book, 2013, 6.

7. Ezra Taft Benson, "Beware of Pride," *Ensign*, May 1989.

8. Gordon B. Hinckley, "Words of the Prophet: You Can Be Forgiven," *Ensign*, Oct. 2001.

9. Joseph F. Smith, "Sermon on Home Government," *Millennial Star*, Jan. 1912, 49–50.

10. Webster's Dictionary.

11. Joseph Smith, *Teachings of the Prophet Joseph Smith*, Salt Lake City: Deseret Book, 1977, 240.

12. John and Kimberly Bytheway, *What We Wished We'd Known When We Were Newlyweds*. Salt Lake City: Deseret Book, 2000.

13. Ezra Taft Benson, "Council to the Saints," *Ensign*, May 1989.

14. Ibid.

15. Heber J. Grant, *Conference Report*, Oct. 1936.

16. Keith McMullin, "Come to Zion! Come to Zion!," *Ensign*, Nov. 2002.

17. Dean Larsen, "Enriching Marriage," *Ensign*, Mar. 1985, 20.

18. Douglas Brinley, *Living a Covenant Marriage*. Salt Lake City: Deseret Book, 2004.

19. Neal A. Maxwell, "Put Your Shoulder to the Wheel," *Ensign*, May 1998.

20. H. Burke Peterson, "Leave It Alone," *Ensign*, Nov. 1993, 43.

21. Marion D. Hanks, *Conference Report*, Apr. 1969, 57.

22. Ezra Taft Benson, "Council to the Saints," *Ensign*, May 1989.

23. Henry B. Eyring, "To Draw Closer to God," *Ensign*, May 1991.

Chapter 16

1. BYU, *Strengthening Our Families*, 98.

2. L. Tom Perry, "Fatherhood: An Eternal Calling," *Ensign*, May 2004, 69.

3. John Taylor, *Journal of Discourses*, 26:112.

4. Orson Pratt, as quoted by Gordon B. Hinckley, "The Lengthened Shadow of the Hand of God," *Ensign*, May 1987, 52.

5. Ezra Taft Benson, "To the Fathers in Israel," *Ensign*, Nov. 1987.

6. See for example Mary Jane Woodger, "Joseph Smith's Restoration of the Eternal Role of Husband and Father," *Joseph Smith and the Doctrinal Restoration*, The 34th Annual Sperry B. Symposium, 381–396.

7. Press conference audiovisual transcript, Mar. 1995, courtesy of the Public Affairs Department, The Church of Jesus Christ of Latter-day Saints.

8. Joseph Smith, *Teachings of the Prophet Joseph Smith*, Salt Lake City: Deseret Book, 1976, 118.

9. Richard G. Scott, "Receive the Temple Blessings," *Ensign*, May 1999, 26.

Chapter 17

1. Gordon B. Hinckley, "Guardians of the Hearth," *Ensign*, Feb. 2012.

2. David O. McKay, *Gospel Ideals*.

3. Boyd K. Packer, *Mine Errand from the Lord*, Salt Lake City: Deseret Book, 2009, 297–98.

4. First Presidency, *Conference Report*, Oct. 1942, 12–13.

5. David O. McKay, *Gospel Ideals*, Salt Lake City: Deseret Book, 1953 453–54.

6. M. Russell Ballard, "The Sacred Responsibilities of Parenthood," *Ensign*, Mar. 2006.

7. Neal A. Maxwell, "Her spiritual antenna on Christian service . . ."

8. BYU, *Helping and Healing Our Families*, Salt Lake City: Deseret Book, 2005, 174.

9. Neal A. Maxwell, "The Women of God," *Ensign*, May 1978, 10–11.

10. Boyd K. Packer, *Mine Errand from the Lord*, Salt Lake City: Deseret Book, 2009, 283.

11. Gordon B. Hinckley, "Walking in the Light of the Lord," *Ensign*, Nov. 1998, 99.

12. Joe J. Christensen, *One Step at a Time*, Salt Lake City: Deseret Book, 1996, 91.

Chapter 18

1. Gordon B. Hinckley, "Daughters of God," *Ensign*, Nov. 1991, 99.

2. Howard W. Hunter, "Being a Righteous Husband and Father," *Ensign*, Nov. 1994, 49–51.

3. Gordon B. Hinckley, "This Thing Was Not Done in a Corner," *Ensign*, Nov. 1996.

4. Ezra Taft Benson, "Counsel to the Saints," *Ensign*, May 1981.

5. Thomas S. Monson, "Abundantly Blessed," *Ensign*, May 2008, 112.

6. Sheri Dew, *The Biography of Gordon B. Hinckley*, Salt Lake City: Deseret Book, 1996, 140–141.

Chapter 19

1. L. Tom Perry, "Born of Goodly Parents," *Ensign*, Dec. 2005.

Chapter 20

1. "Abuse," in *Eternal Marriage Student Manual #3*. Salt Lake City: CES, 2001.

2. Julie B. Beck, "Teaching the Doctrine of the Family," *Ensign*, Mar. 2011, 17.

3. M. Russell Ballard, "What Matters Most Is What Lasts Longest," *Conference Report*, Oct. 2005.

4. Gordon B. Hinckley, *Church News*, Mar. 10, 1997.

Appendix

1. David A. Bednar, BYU–Idaho Devotional, Sept. 11, 2001.

2. Ibid.

About the Author

Robert K. McIntosh and his wife, Susan, live in Santa Barbara, California. They have five children and are fortunate to have twenty-four grandchildren and even one great-grandson.

They have compiled one book together entitled *The Teachings of George Albert Smith*, and Robert is the author of *How Do You Know When You're Really in Love?*